SALARY STRATEGIES

Books by Marilyn Moats Kennedy

OFFICE POLITICS: SEIZING POWER/WIELDING CLOUT
CAREER KNOCK OUTS: HOW TO BATTLE BACK

SALARY STRATEGIES

Everything You Need to Know to Get the Salary You Want

MARILYN MOATS KENNEDY

RAWSON, WADE PUBLISHERS, INC.
New York

Library of Congress Cataloging in Publication Data

Kennedy, Marilyn Moats, 1943–
Salary strategies.
Includes index.
1. Wages.   2. Negotiation.   I. Title.
HD4906.K43   650.1′2   81-40269
ISBN 0-89256-203-X   AACR2

Published simultaneously in Canada by McClelland and Stewart, Ltd.
Composition by American–Stratford Graphic Services, Inc., Brattleboro,
Vermont
Printed and bound by Fairfield Graphics, Fairfield, Pennsylvania

Designed by Jacques Chazaud
First Edition

For my husband,
Daniel J. Kennedy, Jr.
and the lovely Laura

ACKNOWLEDGMENTS

I would like to thank Donna Reimer, my associate at Career Strategies for her help with this project. Without her assistance I'd still be in the planning stages. I would also like to thank my two researchers, Patricia Ann Seifert and Cynthia J. Shaw. Both have been important in gathering both primary and secondary source information. Career Strategies' clients, individual and corporate, have contributed their experiences. Only discretion and a vow of silence keeps me from thanking them by name.

All of the incidents described in this book happened to real people—usually to more than one. All of the names have been changed to protect the foolish as well as the truly victimized. Company names have also been changed. It's important that people learn to investigate company choices themselves, not act on the basis of a very ephemeral "hit" list. Besides, these incidents don't always represent company policy so much as one individual acting in the company's name.

What has been interesting about writing this book has been watching people try to prosper in the 1980s with attitudes from the 1960s and 1970s. Only in the past few months have we seen a growing realization that peace and love, not to mention self-actualization, are outmoded, even quaint, economic strategies.

The real beginning of this book was December, 1980. I was in a local supermarket making a quick run through the cereal aisle when I spied a well dressed woman in her sixties. She was wearing a mink coat circa 1975–1978. She was also filling her cart with enormous boxes of Wheaties. She put six boxes in the cart just while I watched. Some comment seemed called for.

"My goodness," I said, "You must be expecting a great many grandchildren for the holidays."

"No, she said, "I don't have any grandchildren. "These are for me."

Again, some comment seemed called for. I waited. Then she said, "I eat them. I live on Social Security and with high property taxes and utility bills I end up eating a lot of dry cereal in the winter." I must have looked alarmed because she added, "I do have meat once a week."

It turned out that this woman was 65 and newly retired. She had worked 45 years for a variety of companies but had never vested in any company's retirement plan. She was of an awkward age. The retirement reform laws had changed company programs too late. She was not covered. When she retired she got Social Security and supplemented this with about $100 a month interest from a money market fund.

This woman was poor as surely as any welfare recipient living in a more obvious ghetto. Furthermore, she was a member of the working poor. A great many people like to think that work is somehow a method for staving off poverty. Often that is not true. Like this woman you can work your entire life and be poor anyway. It may be a broad social problem but it's also an individual problem.

Basically, it's up to each person to decide how to plan and manage his or her career in uncertain economic times.

Had this woman vested in a company retirement plan she would not necessarily have gotten a generous pension or one guaranteed against any kind of business adversity. There are no guarantees that anyone, male or female, will be protected against poverty.

What happens to you financially is more under your control, now, 10, 20, 30 years from now than you may think. Big Brother lost the last election nationally. If you want to better take care of yourself at 80 it's important to consider the financial and career decisions you make now. Hence this book.

CONTENTS

SALARY STRATEGIES

1

How Your Salary Is Set

Think back to the last time you were job hunting and about to get to the final negotiations. Depending on the size of the organization, you had been through from one to five interviews. You'd met the people you'd be working with and had lunch with some of them. You'd had a tour of the facilities, met with personnel, and been told about the benefit plan. All that remained was to negotiate your starting salary.

You were determined not to go to work for the same money you were making at your present job. If unemployed at the time, you were *fairly* determined not to do this. You definitely wanted more. How much more did you want? (Other than all you could get, of course!) Did you have a definite dollar amount in mind or just a percentage? How did you know how much you could get? That was the problem. The person who was negotiating for the company held all of the cards. He or she knew not only the top dollar the organization was willing to pay, but what you were making now or had made at your previous job. This vastly improved the company's bargaining position. It meant you had to be prepared with a strategy of your own if you were to get more money.

You Say, They Say

The dialogue in salary negotiations is fairly standard. You're asked what figure you had in mind. If you feel fairly sure that you are wanted, you may name a slightly higher figure than you might if you want the job desperately. Unfortunately you and the company's representative are playing cat and mouse. The boss or personnel person is sizing up what he or she can get you to accept and you are trying desperately to figure out what is the most you can get.

As you and your prospective boss or the personnel representative faced off for this all-important negotiating session, you had little hope of formulating a strategy to get the top dollar because you had so little opportunity of finding out—and verifying—what top dollar was. (You had less than a 50/50 chance of knowing what the company would pay). If the company proposed to pay you $2,000 or 10 percent more than you were making in order to persuade you to move, how could you convince them to make it 15, 20, or 25 percent more? In theory you should bargain, but on what basis and how? Why should you be worth more than what was said to be the "going rate?"

In the end you settled for what seemed, on the basis of very little concrete information, "fair." Fair means that what you got was not necessarily what you wanted, but you could not figure out how to convince the company to pay any more.

Up against a conspiracy of silence—the person making the offer is actually challenging you to guess what number he or she has in mind—you are not in a good spot to bargain. You're going to be a victim. This is no way to do salary negotiation in a serious recession. You will never be effective in negotiating for money, either up front or at annual reviews, unless you do three things. First, you have to know how the organization you propose to work for, or your present employer, sets salaries. What are the hidden values and hidden agenda that subvert the so-called salary system? Second, you must have done your homework so that you have almost as much information about what is going on in the market as a whole as the organization does. Third, you must learn how to plan a strategy and negotiate to get what you want. None of this is particularly difficult. None requires that you turn from Mr. or Ms. Milquetoast to a tiger or tigress. Still, you are going to spend significant time doing the most dreary kinds of research: library work and questioning people.

What Is the System?

Let's begin by examining the practices and pitfalls in the systems that control what you get paid now.

Back at the bargaining table, your prospective employer is offering you 10 percent more than you got on your last job. Since you considered yourself underpaid at that job anyway, you wonder if you would not still be paid below market if you took the offer. Your instincts serve you well. The initial offer is below market even though you couldn't know that for sure unless you'd done your homework. The reason is not that the organization is deliberately chiseling (though it could be). What has happened is that this particular organization adjusts its salary ranges once a year in July. (Yearly salary range adjustments are standard for most organizations, especially those with yearly performance and salary reviews. It keeps the system neat.) You are at the end of the period covered by the last increase, though it would be difficult to find this out during the interview. You'd have to have talked to employees.

More Homework

Let's say the job you want is sales representative. In July 1980, the Ecstasy Toy Company moved its ranges up to market, raising them about 12 percent from their July 1979 level. It is now May 1981. Since July 1980 the market range for the job has moved up about 12 percent because of inflation. In July of

1981 the company will again adjust its ranges, but you won't benefit.

As your prospective boss explained, one of the organization's policies is annual reviews. Your first review will be in May of 1982. Because of the timing of your hiring, you come into the organization about 10 percent behind market (1 percent a month times ten months) and you are likely to fall farther behind during the coming year. While the company may raise your salary at your first review and you may get a merit raise, you will not necessarily make up for any cash you've lost in the past. Your raise might be 10 or 12 percent including a merit increase. You should be at the 24 to 30 percent range if you are to keep up with or exceed inflation. This is 12 percent for last year and 12 percent for 1981 plus merit. Even if the company has no commitment to keep employees perfectly even with inflation it would take at least 18 to 20 percent to bring you even with those in the organization whose anniversary is in July, or soon after.

The company obviously should adjust its ranges more frequently to be perfectly current with the market, but the costs of so doing are prohibitive. In effect, the organization would need to adjust its ranges 1 or 1½ percent a month. Keeping managers of all departments abreast of new ranges would make the compensation area the organization's largest, most complex, and least popular department.

The person for whom you will work, usually the one making you the offer, knows that your salary will be charged against his or her budget. The less in the line item called salary expense the better. If the range for the sales representative's job is $22,000 to $30,000, the boss would like to bring you in at $22,000. This would leave plenty of room for you to move up within that range. It would be a $2,000 raise for you, 10 percent, and it would honor the longevity of the people working for the same boss who are earning $30,000 because they've been there 10 years. The boss's side of the equation seems logical.

Finding Market

What you don't know that refutes all of this is that market for the job is now about $23,700. Remember, the $22,000 minimum was set last July and inflation has been virulent since. The organization is counting on your seeing the $2,000 extra as sufficient incentive to change. In fact, $24,000 would be a more likely minimum if you were inclined to agree to the minimum.

If you didn't reluctantly agree to the organization's first offer, you may have a chance to get more money. Managers in most organizations, including some government and nonprofit ones, have some leeway in setting salaries. In most systems, they can bring an employee in at something up to the midpoint. The midpoint is usually halfway between the minimum and the maximum for the range. In this case, it's $26,000. Understand that this is simply the organization's policy, which the manager is supposed to follow.

If he or she is convinced that you are the one person to fill the job, it's possible for the manager to do one of two things. He or she can get the job regraded and pushed up one range. Assuming that the sales representative job covers many people, it's not very practical to expect anyone to put one sales representative in a grade twelve while keeping 34 as grade elevens. He or she can decide to pay you the midpoint ($26,000) or even $28,000 or $30,000. To do this, he or she will probably want to finesse the decision with his or her boss just in case the organization's compensation analysts want to argue. Still, most line managers have the power, if you can convince them to use it. If you are the only sales representative, the manager can change grades more easily if it seems worth it. However, that is rarely necessary. The manager has wide discretion in what he or she will pay. The main constraint won't be policy, but his or her own budget. If there's money in the budget, it's possible.

You need to know as much about the system as possible because when you're negotiating, a favorite organizational ploy is for the prospective boss to say, "The range for this job is set. I can't pay more than the minimum (or the midpoint)." Most candidates cave in and accept the offer, not because they see any merit in this argument, but because they have no counter argument. They shouldn't cave in. The fact that you've been told the policy does not mean there aren't exceptions. It's up to you at that point to revive your selling effort and begin selling the prospective boss all over again. If you're getting the minimum you haven't made much of a sale!

What should be clear by now is that there is no real compensation system that covers all cases and sees that money is distributed fairly. In most organizations the more powerful the manager, the more leeway he or she has in setting salaries. This is especially true if the manager has profit and loss responsibilities, that is, he or she is a line manager. Managers of cost centers, service areas, and so on, have less power and therefore less discretion.

Companies that lack formal systems are easier to negotiate with in some instances and more difficult in others. Lacking a formal system, salaries can be set in a variety of ways, depending on the specific manager, the health of the organization, and which of the following factors may be in play. These factors play a part in a company which has a formal system, but they are less powerful than in organizations with total management discretion.

History

Many companies are more concerned with what they have paid in the past than with today's market salary levels. If $20,-000 got them a sales representative last year, it should get one this year. If an adjustment is to be made, it should be modest. If the organization is facing cutbacks but needs to fill a particular job, it's not unusual for them to preface offers with something like, "This is all we can pay because business is bad," or

"We'd like to do better for you but this is the best we can do."
Depending on the mind set of the candidate, he or she may decide that this refreshing honesty is worth taking less money. He
or she may also run to a more profitable organization. Nonprofit organizations can use this to raise guilt. "We pay less so
that we can help more of the needy. After all, if we paid you
market, we'd be able to help 25 fewer families next year.
Which would you prefer?"

Desperation

Organizations looking for employees, as well as job hunters,
can get desperate. If a manager is desperate for a computer operator, he or she may juggle the budget to pay more to fill that
slot right away. Some companies with managers who intensely
dislike the interviewing process are willing to pay more than
market just to get and keep people more easily. They are willing and able to pay for convenience.

A desperate manager who pays more than market to get an
employee today may decide to take the surplus out of the first
pay review. This should be negotiated upfront when someone
senses that she or he is the last resort, or the desperation bid,
but agrees to go to work for that company.

Compliance

The manager may not want to argue or rock the boat and
may adhere rigidly to the salary guidelines that may have been
set by an outside consultant. He or she may be trying to run his
or her operation by the book. If the manager refuses to deviate
one dollar either way from the formula, beware. Anyone with
so little flexibility could have problems in other areas as well.
This may also indicate that the manager is powerless or refuses
to exercise whatever power he or she has. It's also the sign of an
extreme risk avoider.

Equity

Small businesses, especially, are prone to set salaries by a standard of "fairness" or "rightness." This system usually tests a candidate for potential loyalty and longevity. The manager may even say that what the organization wants to buy is an employee who will be long-term and loyal. If you are interested in the organization, you must be prepared to probe further to find out what loyalty and longevity really mean. Loyalty can be interpreted any number of ways and you need to know if what is wanted is what you can deliver. If you wait until you're on the job, your career there may be short-lived. The loyalty syndrome strikes organizations from one employee to thousands.

Prestige/Glamour

Some organizations are selling prestige. "If you work for us, you work for the leader," they trumpet. They are *selling* this concept to employees, not just bragging to the world at large. Some go for quite elaborate audio-visual presentations which congratulate employees on having picked a winner. You are expected to take less than market, sometimes as much as 5 or 10 percent for the privilege of saying that you work for the best and largest, the industry leader. You will have less luck bargaining under such circumstances because the organization has a track record of getting people to take prestige instead of dollars. This is equally true of very prestigious universities, social service agencies, and foundations. The fact that you can't trade prestige for cash at a bank is your problem.

Glamour may also depress salaries. The communications industry has always paid the neophyte as little as possible because of the aura of working in this field. But even the glamour businesses pay market to groups in short supply, computer people and accountants, for instance.

Surplus

There are more than enough people who do just what you do, probably about as well. The organization knows this, and they are determined to pay as little as possible. Since they have little, if any, interest in holding on to employees long-term, they are not willing to invest in any individual employee. Your efforts to bargain with such an organization will be useless as long as you have so many economic clones. No one school teacher is likely to earn significantly more than any other, regardless of skill or performance, so long as he or she is perfectly replaceable.

Violent Fancy

Sometimes a manager takes a violent fancy to one particular candidate who may or may not realize that this has happened. If the candidate does realize it, he or she may get significantly more money. If not, managers have even been known to up their initial offers unbeknownst to the candidate. This is most likely to happen when the manager has a very specific type of person he or she wants and is disinclined to accept substitutes. If a sales manager has worked out a very detailed profile of the ideal salesperson, he or she is likely to both rejoice and pay more if you appear to be that model in the flesh.

Least of Many Evils

The manager has not been particularly enthused about any of the candidates. You are the least objectionable. Faced with a very lackluster field, the manager works harder and offers more money to fill the job. If he or she gets you, it's salvation from candidates less suitable. This is not wild enthusiasm so much as resignation. In technical fields where competition for talent may be extremely keen, a manager may think that someone with more personality than the office rubber plant would be worth paying for even if that personality does not rival Johnny Carson's.

Clout

You may be well-connected or from a family prominent in the community, which the manager interviewing you knows or knows of. This could be worth more money only because the manager figures you won't take the minimum. It could also result in your not even being considered because the manager wants a more nondescript, less threatening candidate. You might be paid a bit more because you come from a "top" school, however that may be defined. Many organizations pay for the quality of the degree, although they will generally disguise this, if possible, since no one seems too sure that this is a legally defensible requirement.

What must be obvious is that each of these can be at work in your salary negotiations without your being aware. Unless you've collected data on who's been hired in the past and why, you'll be at a disadvantage in trying to figure out what is going on.

Nonfactors

Just as important as those factors that may affect salary negotiations are those that don't uniformly make a difference. Your education and your specific credentials are only valuable situationally. They have no absolute universal value. If the manager you want to work for believes that Stanford graduates are overbearing, you are unlikely to be able to turn your old school tie into an offer, much less into significantly more cash. Somewhere else you may be covered with roses, but not by that particular manager.

Desirable Traits

The fact that you worked for your previous company for many years, displaying loyalty, productivity, and stability may not impress a prospective boss at all. When Elizabeth went for a job interview, she found that her having had only two jobs in 13 years was a handicap. As the prospective boss said, "We want people who are 'movers,' not people who are (appear to be) risk avoiders." Anything that can be seen as an advantage can and will be seen as a disadvantage by someone.

Here are some examples:

Advantage	*Disadvantage*
Stable	Non-risk-taker
Loyal	Not ambitious
Hard-working	Plodding
Well-liked	No backbone
Aggressive	Overbearing
Ambitious	Untrustworthy
Eager to move	Job hopper

Experience

There are many organizations that proclaim that they must train everyone (in their particular way of doing things) from the lowest clerk to the chief executive officer. Therefore, they are most unwilling to pay for what you've learned in other jobs. You can't sell these kinds of organizations on your past successes since they don't see the past as predictive of what you can or will do for them. They are determined to start people at the minimum in a range. If you work out, they may move you up more rapidly, but there's no promise of this.

For example, a sales organization may not value your previous selling experience, even if it's been for a competitor, unless you have been doing it exactly their way. The same can be true of consulting firms which have very specialized ways of presenting study results, making presentations, or selling.

Productivity

Measuring productivity will certainly be a hot issue in the 1980s as every organization scrambles to bring costs in line with productivity. With the Japanese model as goad—greater productivity for lower cost—many managers are paying lip service to increasing productivity. However, what is talked about may not be what companies actually pay for. This is especially true in service businesses where productivity may be very difficult to measure. Is the public relations assistant who writes the most press releases worth more than one who writes fewer? If so, how much more? Are story placements in the media the measure of productivity? Does productivity necessarily mean results? Many people talk about effort as if how hard you worked was equal to or greater than the end result.

Especially in businesses which depend on "feel" even if they say they don't, productivity may be saleable. Some organizations want to buy a particular type of creativity rather than pay for anything done in the past.

What Does Sell?

Then what does sell? How can you get more money if the traditional values don't always sell? We questioned a number of managers after they'd hired a new employee asking each one to describe the people they'd decided to pay more or even broken the range for. They named five factors that do sell or at least sold them:

• *Personality.* "I liked his/her personality. I thought it would mesh with mine." This was far more important than most managers would be willing to admit publicly. Most managers gave enormous weight to someone they liked and thought they could work with easily.

Personality sometimes meant characteristics shared with the manager. "We're both meticulous people," or "We're both very interested in reading, cross-country skiing, dogs, etc." Shared interests seem to create an instant rapport. A manager confident that he or she has found the formula for success in a particular organization is likely to value in others what he or she has thought helped his or her ascent.

• *Old School Tie.* "We both went to Missouri in journalism, and I know what I'm getting." "We both have degrees in electrical engineering from Tech, so we're on the same wave length." Knowing what you are buying, actually reducing the risk of failure, was worth paying for, many managers reported. In most organizations it's difficult, time-consuming, and politically sticky to get rid of people who don't produce, what with warnings, documentation, not to mention personnel department intervention. Getting people who've had the same training or background is a way to buy insurance against failure.

• *Demographics/Lifestyle.* "He or she seems to have the right kind of background to do the job." Managers are sensitive to incongruities which they pick up in interviews. A banker with six children, who is himself under thirty, is not going to be able financially or socially to compete with a colleague with no children and a working wife. An advertising account executive who is obsessed with racing Porsches is not likely to impress the firm's most important client, a very staid but profitable package goods manufacturer. People are willing to pay more for people whose lifestyles are consistent with what has worked before. After all, who knows what reaction the president of the package goods company will have to the Porsche freak? Why take the chance? If clearly the most qualified, the freak may still get the job, but rarely a premium for signing on.

• *Raw Energy.* "I identified her immediately as enormously energetic. She was like an eager race horse. I knew she'd be more productive for us." The impact of an aura of tremendous energy, particularly during the initial interview, is tremendous. Every manager questioned identified high energy as one of his or her preferred characteristics and seriously handicapped those seen as lethargic. Lethargy may not be in the same league as embezzling company funds, but it's certainly mentioned more often and always negatively. Whatever value "laid back" had in the 1970s, it has not carried forward to the 1980s.

• *Sales Ability.* Regardless of the job, most managers told of paying more to those candidates who "really sold me." "I was impressed with her enthusiasm and her ability to sell herself and that's the skill I need in this job." Part of the selling the successful candidate did was to negotiate with the manager. He or she took the most active role possible in saying what he or she wanted and what he or she would give up to fulfill those wants.

First Offer, Final Offer

In talking with people who had gotten more than the first offer, negotiating made all the difference. Those who did not at least hesitate or question the initial offer were thought to agree with the offer. Even if they didn't take the job because of inadequate money, unless they identified money as the problem when they refused the offer, the manager *assumed* that the refusal stemmed from other factors.

Most interesting in our research was that people who were made a flat offer but who asked for more anyway had a 60 percent chance of getting something more than the initial offer, even when they'd been told that that was the organization's "final" offer!

There was no such thing as wasted preparation time in the salary negotiation process. Some people actually tried to figure the dollar value of the time they spent preparing to negotiate. One woman said she figured she'd got just for her first year on the new job about $200 for every hour she spent preplanning her attack—not a bad return on her time!

By now it should be clear that what is said about how salaries are set, regardless of the size of the organization, is quite tentative. For every policy, there is an exception which can be exploited by people who are prepared to do so.

And Now the Exceptions

There are even exceptions and loopholes built into the formal systems themselves.

• *Systems that value education and formal credentials.* They will always overreward people with those characteristics at the expense of people whose practical experience and productivity would seem to make them far more valuable to the organization. These organizations are buying potential more than proven performance. Therefore, those who lack formal education and credentials must be prepared to confront this issue if they want to work for that organization at top dollar. Unless you look at the biases built into the system, you may not understand why you're being paid less for the same job. Shouting discrimination won't particularly help because it's hard to show that pay for potential is illegal.

• *Systems that value length of service.* Sometimes called experience, longevity systems will tend to undervalue results. Unless you can persuade a manager to make up for this bias, your results will not counteract the experience bias. This happens very often to women whose careers were interrupted by family responsibilities. A system that gives great weight to the absolute number of years of experience regardless of quality or kind, will also tend to work against risk takers. Steady service is the ideal.

There is no evidence to suggest that having done a job for ten years will necessarily be better than having done it for five years. Some companies will want to pay the ten-year veteran more.

• *Productivity is difficult and sometimes impossible to measure.* Therefore, it will be unlikely in other than factory piecework that you'll be much rewarded for what you've produced unless there is something tangible as a result.

Knowing how short every salary system is on accuracy, regardless of its alleged science, and how important selling is, it's up to you to preplan any negotiations. In order to do that, you need information. You especially need the kind of information companies are most reluctant to give: information about salary ranges, requirements for classification within one range versus a higher one, and some understanding of the overall philosophy of the person or people who are making the salary decisions. This is true whether you are planning to leave your present employer for a different one or if you are simply looking for an internal transfer. It's safe to say that much of what you want to know, especially about management behavior versus the organization's policies, *won't be in the company employee manual.* It's up to you to ferret out the facts. The next two chapters will provide tools you'll need to do this.

2

The Organization's Game Plan

When David took a job as assistant production manager for a medium-sized manufacturer, he was 30. He'd had seven year's experience with a smaller company with regular salary increases. His new job paid 10 percent more than his old one. Because he wasn't married and didn't think he really needed comprehensive health or life insurance he didn't ask about the company's benefit plan. Two months after he started David was talking to someone from his former company who told him that his old job had been upgraded. It seems no applicant would work for what David had been paid.

As David thought this over it occurred to him that he should find out if he'd gotten his present job because he was the cheapest candidate. He asked his boss. After some hemming and hawing the boss said that David was indeed the only one of seven who had been willing to work for the salary the company offered. "We were afraid we were going to have to raise the offer until you came along," the boss said.

Until that moment David had never thought much about how what he earned was decided. In this respect, he was like three-quarters of the people who work. Of course he wanted to earn more money if he could. It was just that he'd always concentrated on getting the job done and the salary he earned, rather than on what others he knew earned. He'd assumed that the companies he worked for were paying about the same as their competitors. He didn't verify this with his peers because unlike sex and politics, money is a very taboo subject. It simply hadn't occurred to him that comparing salaries with others doing the same job was important and even necessary. The more he thought about it the more he realized that he was probably being underpaid. He decided to try to find out how much he was behind.

Through some contacts he learned that his company's competitors were paying his counterparts from $5,000 to $15,000 more than he was earning. While he'd expected some spread between the highest rate and the lowest rate, the sheer size of the spread staggered him. He was angry, depressed, and miserable all at the same time. It occurred to him that there was much more to getting paid what he was worth or what others were getting than simply finding a reputable company. What he began to realize was that reputable meant different things to different companies. They'd made him an offer. He'd accepted. Did reputable mean a company must save a man from his own ignorance? He began to suspect that he was going to have to take a much more active role in protecting and advancing his own interests.

You, the Commodity

David had never thought of himself as a commodity. To any organization that might hire him he was not himself so much as a set of skills. The organization's obligation was to pay for those skills at a mutually agreed-on rate. If David agreed to work for much less money than anyone else the organization could find, who's problem was that? Certainly it was not the company's. After all, had David gone into a local department store and found a suit for $175 which was identical to a $300 suit he'd seen in four other places, would he insist on paying the clerk $300 because he knew that to be the market price? Certainly not. If anything, David will buy two suits while congratulating himself on his astuteness as a shopper.

Whatever else David learned in college, the art and science of salary research and negotiation had never been part of his education. In fact, the recruiting system at most colleges encourages the new graduate to compare the numbers given him or her *by the different companies,* not to see how the numbers stack up in the market at large. (There's no guarantee that any school's recruiters represent the market.) Since certain companies tend to recruit at certain schools the range of starting salaries could reflect market, above or below. Salary research is limited often to teaching people to ask questions about benefits, job conditions, and advancement. Placement offices rate their own performance by the number of graduates who are hired, not by the quality of training in lifelong job hunting/negotiation they give their clients. After all, what do the parents who've invested $30,000 in a child's education want to hear? The only phrase the majority are interested in is, "I got a job." This is especially true in bad economic times.

You, the Victim

When the same thing happened to Marsha she assumed she was the victim of sex discrimination. "They're paying the men more, I'm sure of it," she said. Her desire for revenge almost got her fired as she began to engage in a very private guerrilla war against her boss, her co-workers, and the organization as a whole. Helpless, or so she thought, to renegotiate her starting salary, she seethed for six months as she looked for a new job.

Like David and Marsha, you might want to ask yourself if you're being paid as much as you should or could be. Facing a continued high rate of inflation (from radical left to radical right economists predict a 12 percent *minimum* yearly increase and the possibility in 1982 and 1983 of 14 to 18 percent), money is more important than it has ever been. Its value is less symbolic today and more concrete.

But whatever happened to the work ethic? What happened to the idea that hard work was rewarded and the competent moved up? The problem is partly inflation, partly changing values, and partly a philosophy of entitlement (if I work here a year, I'm entitled to a raise).

The Rise of Negotiation

Until the late 1970s most people other than very senior executives did not really do much salary negotiation. They generally accepted any reasonable explanation the organization offered to explain why it was paying a particular dollar amount.

People who treat pay rates, whether initial salary or increases, as givens rather than negotiating opportunities are out of touch with economic reality. Whether you are on the lowest rung of the organizational ladder or perched near the top you may discover that you know far less about how your salary is set than you think.

The myth is that some monolithic force known as "they" set salaries. "They won't pay more than $13,500 for a beginner," the interviewer says. Or, "they really insist that you start at the minimum level of the pay range," the manager says. Who is this mysterious "they?" Lots of people assume it's the personnel department, or, if the company is large enough, the compensation analyst. As a matter of fact, however, personnel departments are information gatherers and advisers to top management. They rarely make policy unless what they recommend is what management would have done anyway.

The myth that an identifiable superior employee exists makes a difference in worker attitudes because new hirees assume that if they convinced the employer of their superiority up front, they got more money. This is part of the game. In the first place, most job interviews resemble sorority and fraternity rush parties more than serious negotiations. As the prospect, you talk about the ecstasy of hard work while the prospective boss talks about the blemish-free nature of the company. Picking a superior employee out of that body of superior claims and counterclaims would challenge Solomon. Most ordinary managers don't try. They've long since learned to screen for the norm and to screen *out* the exceptions on both the bad and good ends.

Who Sets Salaries

In fact, then, who decides how much you will earn this year? Are you being paid for past performance, potential, productivity, longevity, education, style, a combination of these or something else entirely? Is there any such thing as salary negotiation or are you evaluated against a universal yardstick and then slotted into a suitable grade? Are you forced to march in lockstep with everyone else in your same kind of job? What is your role in how much you will earn and how often you'll be evaluated?

If you can't answer these questions in detail there's certainly never been a better time to get started on finding the answers. Unless you take a very active interest in your own finances one or most of the following could happen to you.

1. You could learn after a few months on the job that you agreed to work for a much lower salary than you might have gotten, as David and Marsha did. You might work there for three years and never discover you were far below your peers, especially if people in your organization are tight-lipped. You might also find that instead of your boss being grateful for your involuntary nondeductible contribution he or she regarded you as lacking in judgment, not really businesslike. He or she can't help you advance because you're not really "tough-minded about money."

2. You could find yourself having loyally, productively served an employer for ten years only to learn that someone who joined the company last week is earning slightly, or a

great deal, more than you are. The new employee could make 5,000 or 10,000 dollars more. This happens because you have been getting 5, 6, or 7 percent raises while the market rate for your job has been moving up 10, 15, or 20 percent a year. Since you had made a unilateral judgment that loyalty would be rewarded your disillusionment would be tangible. In compensation circles, this is called compression. That means that the company must pay market to get new employees but once on the job they get smaller raises. The result is that the long-term employee is penalized for his or her loyalty because if he or she changed jobs his or her pay would rise dramatically.

3. You could work for a nonprofit organization for 20 years only to realize that over the years your buying power had eroded up to half of what you earned initially even though you had gotten regular raises. The nonprofit had neither the resources nor the commitment to keep salaries in line with inflation or market. They were counting on employees valuing job security more than buying power. They expected, apparently with good reason, to hold on to you emotionally.

4. You could become fully vested in an employer's pension plan only to find that when the company was sold your pension was merged into the new company's and the rules are now different. This would not necessarily violate any laws. Instead of being able to retire at 55 with a certain pension you learn that you cannot retire before 65 without seriously reducing the amount you'll get. If you had never much looked at the pension plan you would not know that nothing about the plan was chiseled in stone, especially since it was wholly subsidized by the company without any contribution by you. You would never have realized that if the company gives pensions, it can also adjust, change, redirect, settle.

5. You could work for an organization for 20 years and when it goes out of business find that you are lucky to get a lump sum settlement on your pension because of the way the plan was set up. If you were 55 with immediate retirement in

mind, it could be quite a blow. You might find that the lump sum was smaller than you had anticipated because part of the plan's assests were in company stock which is now worth much less.

6. It's perfectly possible for you to work 43 years and never vest fully in anybody's pension plan. Not vesting means you are entitled to no pension from that organization when you retire, regardless of age. If you changed jobs no more frequently than once in nine years—hardly a job hopper—you could end up solely dependent on Social Security plus whatever savings and investments you'd managed to amass on your own.

7. If you were counting on an upward adjustment in salaries when your less prosperous employer was bought out by a far wealthier company, you could be surprised when nothing happens. One of the reasons the wealthy parent bought the sick child was the involuntary contributions employees were making to the company's financial picture. This does not involve any kind of discrimination based on sex, race, religion, etc. Everyone is being treated the same. The contribution becomes part of the new owner's capital. Eventually the parent will be forced to adjust salaries but it's inconceivable that the adjustment would cover back wages. If your employer said, "We'll take care of you when things turn around," implying some nice raise in the future, your new employer isn't bound.

8. You could find yourself having negotiated a raise with a boss only to learn that you get no more raises. Under the company's salary system you have "topped out." You are earning the maximum the organization is willing to pay for that particular job. You are earning top dollar for the job you do. Until the company shifts the entire pay scale up to compensate for inflation, you're stuck. The only way to earn more money is to move up a grade.

Until you meet one of these unpleasant realities, you are unlikely to be obsessed with what you earn. At salary reviews, when new employees are hired who do what you do, and when someone leaves for a better-paying job, the subject comes forcibly to consciousness. Otherwise there's a certain receding quality to salary awareness as you get on with the job. This is changing right now as people begin to think about personal finances in a whole new way. What the 1980s seem to promise most people, despite the rhetoric from Washington, is the need to think more seriously and creatively about income as well as outgo.

Getting the Salary Facts

If knowing the facts about what you earn and how you earn it was important before, it's absolutely critical in a nonstop inflation. Your salary may be increased once a year—twice a year if you're especially lucky—but prices go up daily; "compounded daily" as the savings institutions say. However large the percentage increase or dollar amount you may receive, annually or semi-annually, it's never as large as it looks. Added to this, most of us forget that the IRS takes an increasingly larger bite of whatever raises we get as inflation pushes us into higher tax brackets.

Is everyone in this same spot? According to an article in *U.S. News & World Report,* June 9, 1980, p. 50, about one-third of all Americans are covered by indexing. Indexing means that when the Consumer Price Index (CPI) rises, their salaries, pensions, welfare benefits, food stamps, and other types of income are raised to meet the increase. Of the 65 million people who are estimated to be covered, only about 9 million are working or about 14 percent. The rest are different kinds of retirees (principally on Social Security) who receive disability pay or who are part of the food stamp program.

Many companies who were enthused about indexing when a 7 percent annual rise in the CPI was a lot, are pulling back. They have abandoned even the attempt to keep their employees whole against inflation. As one corporate executive said, "We don't try to match inflation for every employee because we can't and, quite frankly, we don't have to. Many employees expect us to even though they don't figure inflation into their budgets. We can always find some good people who think in absolute dollar increases rather than adjusting for inflation. If we indexed, we'd be paying more money for very little additional return." In addition, many companies can't pass along the cost of indexing to their customers. This is certainly true of nonprofit organizations.

Before you can judge where you stand, long before you can change anything should you want to, you've got to find out how your present employer makes salary decisions. Unless you know this, you'll be helpless against a system you don't understand and whose actions you can't predict.

Getting more money at any point is partly a packaging operation. You've got to understand how to package the message to make it sell. You have to understand what an organization will pay for, how approval is granted for deviations from the rules, and most important how to get your boss to help you. Outside the personnel department, and within personnel outside the compensation area, you'd be amazed at how few people understand how salaries are set. If an individual thinks about it at all, the conclusion is simply that like the legal system, some system is at work. That system, of course, is outside the individual's control. In their hearts, most people assume the system is arbitrary, discriminatory, or plainly whimsical. It may be, but not always.

Decisions, Decisions

Whether it's the sole proprietorship that uses part-time, minimum-wage help or the *Fortune* "500" company with hundreds of thousands of employees, salaries are not set arbitrarily. That is, the people who make salary decisions don't *think* they are setting salaries by whim rather than according to a carefully thought-out plan. Each organization has developed, more or less formally, what can be called a compensation philosophy. This philosophy may be developed by a committee or task force that works on the project for two years; an outside consultant who's paid to make decisions and take the heat; or a sole proprietor who's not even aware that he or she has a philosophy. The sole proprietor may simply do what he or she sees as logical.

An individual employee can work for an organization for years and never hear a clear statement of a compensation philosophy. That doesn't mean one doesn't exist. It simply means the individual has never come into conflict with, nor had reason to question, the philosophy. For instance, the giving of annual increases and only annual increases is a policy. The philosophy underlying it would be something to the effect that, "We (or I) think the discussion of money more than once a year has a negative effect on employee and/or management morale. It's easier for us to manage our own finances if we only have to consider our salary policies once a year. Therefore, we will only review salaries once a year."

Noblisse Oblige

When Jack went to work for the largest bank in his city he was warned by the personnel director that he must never discuss his salary either in general or specific terms with any other employee. (The bank couldn't do anything about salary discussions outside the bank, or maybe they hadn't thought to include it in the policy.) To do so was grounds for immediate dismissal. (This has since been ruled an unfair labor practice by the National Labor Relations Board, 217 NLRB 122). Furthermore, Jack was told any discussion about money must be initiated by his boss. He was never to bring the subject up himself. That was the policy. The philosophy behind it goes something like this. "I (or we) own this bank. As a reward for the risks we've assumed in providing employment for people, we are entitled to treat what we pay them as our exclusive perogative. We can set salaries as we see fit and we do not seek, nor will we tolerate, any unsolicited input from the beneficiaries of our largesse. Furthermore, discussions among employees about money could encourage people to put more emphasis on money than on work itself or they might find out that we are setting salaries arbitrarily."

Cost Plus

The owner of a local computer service company decided on a very simple salary policy. He believed that the best way to set salaries was to start low. Therefore when he interviewed a prospective employee he always insisted that the person tell him what he or she made on the last job before he'd discuss money. He then asked if 5 percent more would be satisfactory. If not, he'd go to 10 or even to 15 percent. It tickled him to discover that the more eager the candidate, the lower the price. His game was to make the prospect bargain for every dime. The employee who bargained hardest was naturally the shrewdest and therefore worth the extra money. His philosophy was an extension of his own entrepreneurial bent in that he saw each employee as essentially self-employed and responsible for his/her own fortunes. "If an employee thinks he or she is worth more, I will pay more."

Me, Too

Another company set salaries by looking in the Sunday newspaper want ads. When they found what competitors were paying for the same sort of jobs they would match the offers. If the prospect questioned this, they would cite the competitor's offer. The philosophy simply stated was, "We shouldn't have to pay more than anyone else and we probably can't get away with paying less."

Luxury Sweatshop

The largest tool manufacturer in one Sun Belt city prided itself on its philosophy of paying the highest rate for the highest productivity. It ruthlessly pruned people who didn't closely match the highest level of productivity attained by any one person on the line. Not limited to blue collar workers, it also pruned any managers seen as falling behind their peers. The philosophy was, "We pay dearly to get the last ounce of effort out of our people, and we keep sorting them out until we have only the most productive ones." It was not difficult for a union to win a certification election despite management's surprise, dismay, and eventually spirited resistance.

A Little Here, a Little There

The clothing store paid the minimum wage, but sweetened this with a 20 percent discount. The discount applied not just to the clerk's clothing but on gifts, clothes for family, friends, etc. The clerks frequently bought things for friends and neighbors and split the 20 percent savings with them. The store didn't care because it's philosophy was that any clerk was pretty much like any other clerk. The important task was to keep the sales slots filled with warm bodies. Also, since most retailers marked merchandise up at least 50 percent and more often 100 to 150 percent, this was actually an aid to the selling effort.

In addition to its conscious or unconscious philosophy every organization has a written or oral policy of how and why wages for employees are set at a particular level. Sometimes the real reasons are lost in the misty past though the policy continues in force. No one at Jack's bank could explain why employees were not supposed to discuss money with each other, although there was plenty of speculation and none of it was favorable to the management. Punishment for violating the policy was swift and terrible if you believed company legend which, Jack was told, few cared to bet against.

The philosophy of an organization is very important and often influential because it gives management a reason, in some cases a justification, for its policies. It reduces the apparent level of arbitrariness employees see in the way salaries are determined. It gives individual supervisors and managers ways of explaining the illogical. Knowing the philosophy of the company can be useful if you want more money because you can develop a strategy likely to work in that environment. In fact, this must be a starting place in developing a successful strategy.

How the Theory Came About

In theory, differences in salaries are supposed to respond to four significant differences in jobs. These are the level of *skill* needed to do the job, the *effort* that must be expended, the level of *responsibility* the job entails, and the *working conditions* the employee must contend with. A person who digs out septic tanks for a living should earn more money than someone who digs under less unpleasant conditions. Night factory work usually pays more than the same work done during the day. Even in informal employment situations these factors are important. A baby sitter charges more for four children than for one.

Important as these four factors are, they do not of themselves determine how much a particular kind of job pays. They can be superseded by the market. A computer operator in a very pleasant office may make much more than someone with greater skill, expending much more effort, with a higher level of responsibility, and under dreadful working conditions. Think about the pay for the average teacher in an inner city school versus a computer programmer. With the same level of education the programmer will make more money because the market is better for programmers than for teachers. We will look more closely at market in a minute.

When there are measurable differences in effort and results on a job being done by several people, a compensation system should reward the people or the individual doing the most work. This is called a merit system. If everyone is paid exactly the same rate, regardless of productivity, there is a lack of merit or what companies call internal equity. Internal equity also covers the relationship between different kinds of comparable jobs as well as the relationships between people doing the same job. If one group of employees are seen to do less but receive more money, others will see this as a lack of internal equity. The theory is that the dissatisfied ones will, in the long run, move on to other jobs. Most companies show great enthusiasm for the idea of a merit system.

Two Wage Theories

In classic compensation (wage/salary) theory, every job in a company is compared with every other job for purposes of deciding how much to pay for each kind of job. This can be done in a number of ways but the two most common methods are ranking and classification/slotting. Ranking is probably the oldest, most logical, and the easiest method. Whoever is in charge of making money decisions simply puts all of the jobs in order of each job's overall value to the organization, from most valuable to least. If sales managers are more important than assistant sales managers they'll be ranked higher. If secretaries are more valuable than draftsmen, they'll be ranked higher. Note that this is purely internal and takes no notice of external competition for workers of a particular kind.

This method works very nicely in organizations that don't have hundreds of jobs and when there are clear differences between the perceived value of jobs. The differences must be clear to employees lest they decide that what they are paid is unfair vis-à-vis some other job and seek employment elsewhere. Turnover is the ultimate long-term expression of employee dissatisfaction.

The second method, classification, groups different kinds of jobs into grades. This is very common. Civil service is a kind of classification method with grade levels. Many companies have developed their own classification system, or hired consulting firms to do so. This method rates the value of groups of jobs in relationship to other groups of jobs. Instead of one job category, (e.g., secretary) being paid one rate or having one range, secretaries, key punch operators, and draftsmen may be grouped together in one range. The problem is that someone must decide on the number of classifications, rank them in order as in the ranking system, and decide on pay ranges. They must also decide how much difference or overlap there will be between ranges. The concept of a pay range was covered in greater detail in Chapter 1.

There are other job classification systems that use point plans. If a job has a great many points, it is a higher paying job. If fewer points, a lower paying job. The factors chosen and the way they are rated are decided on in advance so that while such a system seems fairer, it's just as dependent on judgment as ranking or classification.

The factor comparison method uses factors that are supposed to be fundamental to all jobs and that seem to apply across the board. For instance, how much manual skill is required for different jobs? Longevity, education, or experience may be measured with points given for quality and quantity. No one of these systems has any claim to objectivity. Each is tailored to what the people who control the organization value. Sex, age, and race discrimination can be built into the system or filtered out but will not necessarily be present or absent because of the system.

So far the company has worked internally, almost in a vacuum, in deciding on salaries. None of these systems can work until the organization has looked at the market value of the jobs it wants to fill. *Market value means the dollar amount that most, an average, or a combination of companies using the same kind of talent pays for a particular job or kind of job.* Someone within an organization may decide that secretaries are far more valuable to that particular organization than key punch operators or that senior secretaries are far more valuable than junior sales support people. That decision is irrelevant if the market dictates that key punch operators aren't to be had for fewer dollars than secretaries and that sales support people insist on 20 percent more than senior secretaries. A company may have to try its system in the market place to find out what it wants is not available at the price it will pay.

The market is more influential than either company philosophy or internal company systems in setting salary levels because if a company falls too far behind the market in its salaries, it may get no people at all! However, there will always be people who will work for a wage below market. They may not be willing to work indefinitely for the lowest paying employer in the region, but they may work for organizations that pay below the average. Some will do so out of ignorance, some because they do not want the hassle of making a thorough job search. Some will like the person who interviews them, feel comfortable, and end the search immediately. As with David and Marsha however, the honeymoon may be short. There is no greater work-related disillusionment than to find you have agreed to work for less money than you might have gotten.

In the past a great many companies felt that the simplest way to keep the majority of employees happy was to use a system in which everybody doing the same job started within a few hundred dollars of each other and in which longevity was rewarded more often than merit. If the company paid competitively, keeping people would be no problem. The idea was that most employees would rather forego significantly more money than other employees if the reverse would not be true. They valued the golden mean. As long as the senior employee made the most money everyone could see when he or she would make the most for a particular job.

This approach to salary setting meant that it was difficult for a superstar, outside sales or an area in which productivity was very measurable, to show that he or she was a superstar and be rewarded for it. If the organization wanted to keep a star it would kick him or her up a grade, changing the job title and the job description in the process. This meant that eventually the grade system was so distorted that it really had been destroyed.

In some organizations, bonuses were given that recognized extra performance or effort while leaving the relationships between jobs unchanged. That way, if a particularly productive employee moved far ahead of his or her competitors and eventually left the company, that job would revert to the normal pay range. There would be no need to start the new worker at the salary the star had earned when he or she left.

Old Values, Old Style

The "greatest good for the greatest number" worked fairly well in organizations in which productivity could not be accurately measured or in which people worked very hard and were very productive because they personally chose to do so irrespective of who they worked for or what they earned. For instance, the manager who always worked Saturdays and whose troops also worked Saturdays, even though there was no extra money involved, did so as a matter of choice. There was an investment in the job and a pride in it which was not necessarily compensated for nor expected to be.

When inflation was much lower, people could afford to worry more about what they did than how they were rewarded. In 1981 they don't feel that way at all. Many people have developed an independent philosophy about salaries, which might be called *entitlement*. In essence, entitlement says, "If other people get raises annually, I should too whether I produce more or not. If I am not fired and I still breathe, I deserve a raise." For many people it is the organization's responsibility to keep them whole against inflation. When inflation was about 6 or 7 percent some companies did attempt to keep employees even. In a 12 to 18 percent annual inflation, very few are still trying. Naturally, if enough organizations adopt this philosophy the market rate for many jobs won't increase to match inflation.

The entitlement philosophy bumps heads with the organization's philosophy that a job has an absolute value to the organization. If the range for senior engineers is $35,000 to $50,000 but you've been in the job for so long that you're now making $50,000, you have a problem. Even if others in the department are getting 12 percent raises you're not likely to get anything until the market value of the job causes a shift upward in the range. You have topped out. You can't expect to get more money except as the organization responds to market.

If there is so much talent available that you are easily replaceable, you may not get an across-the-board increase. If the radio station for which you work has thirty unsolicited, highly qualified applicants for your job every week, the management may see little need to pay you more. You can be replaced by someone equally competent at the same or a lower figure. In fact, turnover is a good thing because if each employee stays only a year there is no need to give annual raises. The salary remains permanently at one level.

The rogue factor in all this is that most systems have lots of leeway. You aren't necessarily at the mercy of a system because the elasticity of the system means you can position yourself more than one way. Your boss can work for or against you depending on your ability to sell and negotiate. Knowing what the organization thinks it's doing is important, but you also need to see what happens to any one individual. Even though you are only one individual and the company appears to hold the better cards, you are not powerless. You can often combat management strategies by getting information as good or better than that management uses for its decisions.

3

How to Determine
Market Salary Level
for Your Job

There is no more burning issue for most of us than whether
we're being paid as much as we think we should or could be.
Before you try to negotiate or renegotiate anything with anybody, you need to know if what you are paid now for what you
do is market.

Market means market price. People's services are not much
different than hamburger when it comes to pricing. If the
A & P, Kroger, three regional chains, and four "Mom and
Pop" grocery stores charge within a dime plus or minus $2.06
per pound for hamburger, $2.06 is the market price for ham-
burger on that day. Food prices have even less stability than
people prices and tomorrow's market may by $2.13 plus or
minus eight cents. The plus or minus means that plotted on a
graph the midpoint of the range is $2.06 and the lowest anyone
is charging for hamburger in that city is $2.06 − .10 or $1.96
and the highest is $2.16.

With the pricing of people there is a funnel distribution.
Clerks and typists may vary only a few hundred dollars per

year from the midpoint while chief executives may vary thousands on either side.

The geographic area may be countrywide or international for top management versus a twenty-mile radius for clerks. If people with your same or very similar skills, education, and experience are mostly clustered at $15,500 and you're making $16,500, you are probably at or may even exceed market. If you're making $13,500, there's a problem.

Lots of organizations tell employees that they can't compete with a particular type or size of organization because that company has "inflated" salaries. It may be true that they can't or won't compete for your job, but for jobs in which labor is scarce (programmers, engineers, nurses, etc.), the stingiest organization is paying at or near market. Otherwise they would not have any people in those categories at all!

Because of the way it's figured, market operates independently of what any one company pays. Most companies with any kind of compensation sophistication or those concerned about their competitive positions make annual or biannual salary surveys. Some do this for every kind of job, others for key jobs within each range, planning to adjust the range for all of that kind of job.

Unfortunately how much research a company does depends more on how many people they have to do it rather than strictly on need to know. The decision to do extensive research may be based on turnover. If the place needs revolving doors in personnel to keep traffic in and out moving smoothly, top management may want much more data. No genius is required to deduce that, particularly in a recession, salaries out of line with the market increase turnover. No two salary experts agree at what level one particular underpaid employee will seek employment elsewhere. As a group, however, a majority of people will think about job hunting for a 10 to 20 percent increase. Turnover costs money especially within groups of scarce skills.

What Are the Facts?

Let's look first at what kind of data a company assembles. Then we'll see how much of this you can get access to at not too much trouble or expense. Keep in mind that salary information is supposed to be top secret. God forbid the employees find out where they really stand.

Organizational paranoia about salary information cuts across all sizes and types of organizations. Even if a company publishes or posts union scales, it may fiercely guard the non-union scales. From tiny to mammoth, organizations would prefer that employees and prospects know few specifics beyond what each one will make. After all, it would be next to impossible to get any help if pay checks were a total surprise until someone began working at the job!

Depending on the size of the organization, a company can do anything from calling one competitor and asking very specific questions or offering to trade information, to running a full-scale survey with data collected and analyzed by a consulting firm. Most compensation analysts agree that for any kind of accuracy more than one source of data must be used. The risks are too high to use only government figures or those of a direct competitor.

Whatever the organization chooses to do, its object is to establish the entry level salary, not just a range, for each of its principal kinds of jobs. Entry level is the figure at which a new employee will start regardless of where he or she does so. Because such surveys are both costly and time consuming, most organizations will collect data only on those job categories with many workers or in which they are having difficulty with recruiting or turnover. If the labor market in a particular area is very "hot" right at the time, they will spend more effort getting accurate data. If the market is fairly depressed with people willing to work for current rates, they may do little research or skip it entirely. If personnel can't even process all the qualified applicants, money is no problem. If there have been layoffs based on seniority, the entire survey would be out of balance because it will reflect the much higher salaries of long-term workers. It will be hard for a company to say what it would pay a new recruit when it can't hire any.

Your information needs and the organization's are never identical. You need to know at any time you want to change jobs, whether internally or externally, what the market is, regardless of the competition for the job. You must find out what your clones are being paid fairly specifically. Remember that our goal is to stay whole against inflation, not just to get a raise when moving from one spot to another.

The best sources of information for organizations, and generally for you, are the following. You'll have to use more undercover methods to get information, but it can be done, as you'll see.

• *Competitors.* How much are an organization's direct competitors paying for someone doing the job you are doing? When companies do surveys of competitors they are very careful to define very specifically what information they want. That way they are comparing apples with apples, not apples with tangerines. They will usually ask for the following: (1) actual base salaries; (2) typical overtime earnings; (3) bonus/cash profit sharing; (4) salary range for positions; (5) entry rate, selection criteria, and any other benefits that might affect the organization's competitive position. This might include something like company parking, subsidized food, or fully paid medical and dental care. They don't want a ball park figure that some companies call "starting salary" because unless it's broken down, they can't do accurate comparisons with other companies.

Do competitors give accurate information or do they change salaries to protect image, competitive position, etc.? Most claim they give accurate information in the hope of getting the same back. However, as one compensation analyst pointed out, "We would never rely on competitive information alone. We always compare it with three or four other sources. Salary data is so sensitive you can't predict what people will do."

In order to do a comprehensive job of gathering information, most companies will not match themselves strictly with clones, that is, companies that are identical in size, product lines, etc. They will look at nonprofits, small companies, service businesses, units of state, local, and federal government, who would compete with them for people. This is a broader interpretation of competitor, but all of these groups do compete with your organization for talent.

• *Governmental Survey Data.* The federal government, through the Bureau of Labor Statistics (BLS), provides a variety of survey data on salary levels for different kinds of jobs. Depending on the date at which data was gathered, not when the report was issued, you must adjust for inflation. You can call the local office of BLS and ask for reports on recent salary surveys in the geographic areas you're interested in. Some of this information is free, for some there is a nominal charge.

Some local governmental units do area wage surveys. These mostly survey blue collar people, but occasionally data are collected for professional and technical people as well. Again, you must watch the age of the data and adjust the rates for inflation. Any area development council charged with bringing new employers into the area should have some survey data. Check its age.

• *Trade/Professional Association Surveys.* These are among the most useful both to companies and to individuals. Many associations run annual salary surveys of all members or a sample of the membership. The most sophisticated of these will be adjusted for region and type of company with very detailed descriptions of particular kinds of jobs. The American Society for Personnel Administration runs such a survey which asks people in particular kinds of organizations to fill out an extensive survey. This compilation gives valuable salary information at all levels but is especially useful to people moving from one section of the country to the other.

It has been argued that people can lie about what they earn on a survey. People can *always* lie about anything. Our experience has been that there's very little ego gratification in lying because it's all anonymous.

There are also surveys run by the American Management Associations (30 different surveys), Administrative Management Society, Bank Administration Institute, Women in Communications, Inc., and hundreds of other organizations. It's worth your time to go to the library and use the Gale Research Company listing of business and professional associations or *National Trade & Professional Associations*. Find the one, or several associations which seem closest to your job interests. Contact them about their surveys. Some publish an overview of the results in one of their publications. Others expect members who need detailed information to purchase the complete report. (It's always possible to find someone who did buy it and just borrow it.)

• *Consulting Organizations/Survey Firms.* Organizations with money to spend and a compelling need to know can engage firms that survey particular markets or even every kind of position one organization might have. Some of the best known are A.S. Hansen, Inc.; Hay Associates; Hewitt Associates; Organization Resources Counselors, Inc.; Cole, Warren and Long, Inc.; D. Dietrich Associates, Inc.; and Battelle Memorial Institute. You, unless you are just faking a need for money, can't afford to buy this information. You can find friends and acquaintances in organizations with access to this data and see if someone won't let you in on what has been reported for a particular category.

Sometimes these firms release bits of national surveys they've done to the *Wall Street Journal* as part of an overall public relations effort. It's worth a look at the business index to see if the *Journal* or a similar publication has covered information about your particular occupational family.

• *Newspaper Want Ads.* Some companies employ "checkers"

to verify that the salaries being advertised in want ads are indeed what the company is prepared to pay. Small companies may even chart the want ad salaries for certain kinds of jobs looking for an average rate or the midpoint.

For individuals this can be a problem unless you can find someone within the organization to verify the actual base salary. Most reputable companies only publish actual ranges, but there are those who inflate as a come on.

Other Sources

There are other sources of salary information that you can tap and employers probably wouldn't.

• *Search Firms/Employment Agencies.* Sometimes these sources will give you accurate information whereas they might inflate starting salaries were they talking to potential clients. The accuracy of the data will depend on the integrity and first-hand knowledge of the person you talk with. Again talk to more than one. It is not always in the best interest of the firms to give accurate information, especially if they think you are a potential placement candidate. You can use them as one source of information, never as the only source. In our survey, the tendency was for a recruiter to inflate salaries if you were a desirable candidate and to suggest that you would be lucky to get in at all if they had no openings in that category. The most knowledgeable people in this area are those who deal with only one career area or one industry because they are usually informed in depth on both the different kinds of jobs and what each entails plus they do enough business in that area to keep track of market movements.

• *Surveys run by local chapters of trade/professional associations.* If you want to get a firm figure on market for a particular kind of job in your city, check the local branch of a trade/professional association. Many run these surveys to keep members abreast of what they should seek at annual salary reviews.

The larger the organization, the most likely it will be to have done such a survey.

• *Talking with individual members of trade/professional associations who do about what you do.* It's not politic to ask someone exactly what he or she makes when it's known that the two of you are competitors or potential competitors. In fact, salary information is the last frontier of privacy. You will find people talking about sex in the most graphic detail at cocktail parties, but asking someone to tell his or her salary will make you a social outcast. It's the ultimate taboo. Knowing how people feel about telling anything about income, you've got to get them to share company data with you in salary ranges or grades. It will be almost impossible to get the last dollar offer an employer made for a particular kind of job. What you can get, however, is the pay range for the job and the likelihood that the offer was at the minimum, below the midpoint, or higher than the midpoint. The latter is usually set by tradition or policy.

One of the ways you can get cooperation out of the reluctant and insure some degree of accuracy in your results is to treat this as a full-scale research project. Select the companies you want to know about, settle on a range of jobs to be investigated, and find contacts in those organizations. If you promise to share the results with them when you get them, you will be amazed how much help you get. People talk about the "ethics" of such a survey only when they think you want them to help. We have never met anyone who didn't want to insure that he or she was getting the top dollar wherever he or she worked. By the way, promising to share the results is how companies get each other to share such sensitive data. Why not use the same principle with individuals?

Companies, as we said, frequently need and want entry level salary data for a wide variety of jobs. They may also want range information; median, midpoint, and average data; and lots of other technical data. None of this is as important to the individual as it is to the company because you are not going to do any sophisticated statistical analysis on your information. What you are going to do is construct a scatter graph like the one shown below.

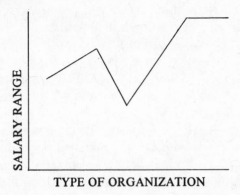

You will learn two things. You will find out what kind of organization pays what level salary as well as which individual company pays a particular salary. You will also see what the overall maximum and minimum market range for a particular job is in your area. In some areas, such as teaching, data processing, and government jobs the range may be very small. In some kinds of management jobs the range may be as much as $20,000.

The Walk-through

Let's assume that you've talked to a number of organizations about a public relations job, variously called Press Relations, Publicity Director, and Associate Manager of Public Relations. This is not an entry level job, neither is it strictly management. You fit in a "professional" category. You've talked to both a small and a large public relations agency, the PR department of both a large and a small company, and a university. This is probably more than you'd actually do unless you were surveying the market at a rather leisurely pace. Most people choose a job from no more than three possibilities, according to our research. You have not had an offer from any of them, but you think that one or two are getting close to that stage. In the final negotiating process you are likely to be asked how much money you have in mind. What will you say?

You call several employment agencies and find that the range may be anything from $15,000 to $25,000. That's much too wide to give any of these prospects as your range. Ordinarily the range should be $2,000 or $3,000, not $10,000. A very broad range signals the employer that you really don't have a clue about market.

You have about a week to do your research because you have an interview with the large company scheduled for one week from today. You might be asked to name your range then so you must be prepared. You go to your research file and find that all you have are names of some people you've met in the past. You begin to fill in your graph. Since the only concrete information at this point is $15,000 to $25,000, you will start with that. Working in increments of $1,000, you'll fill in the numbers up the left side of the chart. Now you need something across the bottom. This axis will have the names of the different organizations in your survey.

You decide that the only government data available to you is

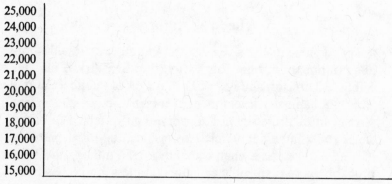

much too old to be valuable. You'd need an M.S. in mathematics to bring it up to date and that could be inaccurate because the inflation rate wasn't consistent from month to month. Best to begin telephoning.

You telephone the membership chairman of the publicity club in town or the local branch of PRSA (Public Relations Society of America) and ask who she or he knows who does the kind of job you are interested in, variously known as Press Relations, or Assistant Director of Publicity. The membership person gives you five names from the directory. You call each of them and explain what you're trying to find out. You offer to share your research when it's done. You and they know that what you're asking for is what they started at, if it was recently or what they believe the organization would pay for the job you've described if it were to be filled tomorrow. You maintain the fiction that it's not their personal salary you're interested in but a range. Out of the five people you talk to probably three will give you something concrete, if only because they may be job hunters soon or are now and they want to insure reciprocity.

Salary Research Traps

Here's where salary researchers fall into a trap, not just individuals, but companies too. Remember our talk about comparing job characteristics? Don't let your source off the hook, despite the fact that this conversation is causing both of you to have premature hot flashes, until you cover the basics. These include: (1) some description of the job responsibility; (2) job grade, relative to others in the department, that is, is it in the middle of the PR jobs, the lower end, the higher end; (3) education and experience required or desired; (4) any special benefits included—remember that pay may be lower if there are some noncash benefits that employees are likely to value; (5) as much other information about what specific duties are involved as you can get. Remember that everything is relative. If there are many similar jobs below this one in the same area, it's probably a higher level job, if not, possibly lower level. Some of these decisions will be personal ones based on comparing each company's information with every other's.

Keep in mind that this isn't science, no matter who's gathering the information. Like the *Washington Post* reporters looking for clues in the Watergate scandal, you've got to get several people whose estimates are close before you can have any confidence in your data.

Once you've talked to your professional sources, try to locate some contacts in each of your target organizations. Anyone who can put his or her hand on the job posting announcement will be invaluable. Job posting has been a great help to salary researchers because part of the posting process in most organizations is to give the salary grade for the job, if not the actual salary range. If you're looking at very small organizations, you probably won't find anyone with access to the real numbers unless you know someone well enough who can go into the person who's hiring and ask him or her what range he or she has in mind. Small companies are rarely involved with formal job posting. You're also more likely to find small companies depending on the *candidates* for information!

If you are trying to find out what the range is for a job within your own organization, depending on size, job posting may be a factor. Just because it's an internal transfer doesn't mean that your own organization might not be persuaded to pay more if you could prove it didn't meet market. Remember management discretion. Someone must initiate a review of the range and who would benefit more from an upgrading than you? You are essentially doing the work of the personnel department, but as long as you get what you want, who cares?

When you're trying to get information internally, you have to be as light as an 80-pound ballerina. Otherwise, you'll disturb the whole office structure. The reason companies say they don't want employees talking about money too much is that they are afraid they'll be besieged by requests for salary changes. Don't you believe it! They are far more worried about employees finding out how wide the disparity is between pay for the same job, even in the best managed and presumably most equitable companies. Make your inquiries as discreet as possible. It's better to suggest a range, "Do you think the job would be between $15,000 and $20,000 or between $18,000 and $22,000?" Give people alternatives to choose from rather than forcing them to come up with the numbers themselves. Most people are more comfortable if they have to agree or disagree rather than state facts or suppositions.

Some information will be in the grapevine, but it may be distorted by two factors. Only the most outrageous extremes get reported by enough people to be easily reached cross department through the grapevine. The extremes may be too much so. Second, numbers travel poorly through the vine because what the vine does best is impressions, not exact statistics or time tables. The grapevine may also transmit news of your interest. This may not be at the time you'd like to play your hand. Extreme caution is called for.

Protective Coloring

One of the arguments for continued salary research is that if you are always on the lookout for information, nobody sees your interest as a heightened one. You're known to be interested in all kinds of jobs, not just your own. This is not a bad reputation to have because it provides such excellent protective coloring. Nobody knows what your game plan is because you are simply perpetually in action.

At this point you have one other major source of information you need to tap if your initial five contacts didn't provide it. You need to check with what your prospects' closest competitors are paying. If you're looking at four prospects, who are their competitors? Track down a contact in each place and ask who the organization's nemesis is. If you've been working for your present employer very long, you know who is a major competitor.

If you work for the largest bank in town, the second largest bank is on your heels in every way, including salaries. How about the savings and loan? It's a competitor for financial talent, too. Are there any other financial institutions or advisory services who use people with your skills? Widen your definition of your industry.

By now you should have a diagram which looks more like this.

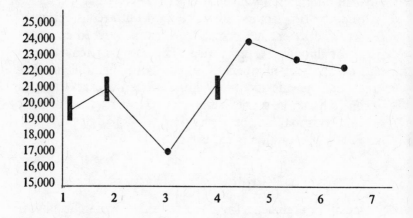

1. Fortune "500" company with huge department
2. Direct competitor of company you now work for
3. Nonprofit agency
4. Trade association salary survey
5. Bureau of Labor Statistics or area economic survey
6. Very profitable small company
7. Very profitable medium-size company

You are now ready to connect the bars and see what you get. You'll notice that most of the organizations you researched came in between $19,000 and 23,000. Only one lonely nonprofit hit below $19,000. Since you're talking to a university, this is important. If you were only talking to companies, you might drop out the nonprofit although strictly speaking it's in competition for talent with the companies you're interested in.

Critical Questions

Now that you've found the probable range and you have some confidence in your numbers, you are ready to think about the numbers you'll mention when asked. There are two other considerations that must be included before you settle on your personal range.

What did you make on your last job or what are you making now? If you are making $19,000, it wouldn't be particularly helpful to change jobs at $19,000. That won't boost you. If the range is $19,000 to $23,000, you'll have to talk in terms of a range of $22,000 to $24,000. You should make the bottom number of your range whatever your minimum number to move is. If you don't, you may be asked to take the minimum of whatever range you set. About 50 percent of the time if your range is close to the company's range, you'll get the minimum you ask for. Managers have a bent toward the lowest number you say regardless of range.

What are the pension rights and vesting procedures? Unless you have developed an inordinate fondness for poverty, you might be willing to make certain tradeoffs between pension benefits and immediate cash. As we have said, every time you get a raise, you move to a higher tax bracket. Often pension plans provide future income without the present tax obligation. There are still a few, usually smaller companies, with pension plans that provide for vesting after the first year or 18 months, not the 10 years maximum the law provides. It may be worth moving your range down for that particular employer. Profit sharing, particularly if there is no formal pension plan, means that you can set up your own IRA (Individual Retirement Account). This is probably the best of all possible worlds because it's under your exclusive control and tax deferred. If the profit sharing or annual bonus is large enough, an employer without a pension plan is preferable. Don't ignore the small company if you must move around! Their assets may be more portable!

Always keep in mind that it's very difficult in the current business climate to guarantee that both you and the company will want to continue your relationship for 10 years. Many marriages don't last 10 years and the process for firing a spouse is infinitely more complicated and costly! You may actively search for an organization whose pension plan is nonexistent or has a shorter vesting period.

Maximizing your dollar value as an employee does not mean that you must always get the last dollar up front, although that's usually best. Remember the progressive tax rate. Your earning more doesn't mean you take home proportionately more. What is important is to look at the relationship between cash, pension options, if any, and benefits.

We saved benefits for last because they usually have the least cash value and the least influence on employment decisions. Benefit packages have traditionally favored men with families. There has been more emphasis on life insurance, usually term, health insurance, and disability. Two of the three are most valuable to married people generally, and specifically to married men. Health insurance is important to everyone. A company which structures its benefit plan for married men is less likely to see the particular needs of single women. Women with dependents may be more interested in life and disability insurance. Whatever your situation, you need to count in your compensation package only those benefits you can use. If you are single, of either sex, you may not have anyone you want to enrich with $100,000 worth of life insurance. On the other hand, you may be able to use a college tuition remission plan, especially if it pays for everything. It would take a healthy pretax raise to make up for the nontaxable $2,000 a year in tuition a company offers or could be persuaded to offer.

Evaluating Benefits

Most organizations have a basic benefit package that usually includes life and health insurance. Some offer only a partially paid health insurance plan. If you are covered by health insurance now which you pay nothing for, it will be difficult to figure how much you'd have to pay for the same coverage were you to supply it yourself. Therefore, you need another table.

Benefit	Yr. Company	Company A	Company B	Company C
Life insurance $100,000	480	50,000, 240	$200,000 Accidental $1,000	None

You must figure what it would cost to buy each benefit if you were solely responsible for paying for it yourself. Unless you compare replacement costs your choices will be restricted to those organizations that offer roughly the same benefits as you now have. Most personnel departments can tell you the replacement value of what the organization offers. This is not the same as the amount the organization pays because it almost always gets a group rate for which you aren't eligible. If not, check with the carrier who issued the policy. If it's a group policy from insurance company A, call them and ask them what it would cost you to carry that policy on your own.

Don't forget the other fringe benefits that are company policy. If one company offers two weeks vacation the first year while another offers only one, you'll have to "buy" an extra week (maybe as unpaid leave if that's even possible). That's more money from company A. If company B subsidizes its food service operation more than 50 percent and another has none at all, you'll have to talk in terms of the cost of eating in the local tarnished spoon or bringing your own lunch.

If this seems incredibly picky and time consuming, keep in mind that it is your money we're discussing. How much is it worth to you to maximize what you earn? The worst thing that can happen to you is to change jobs for what you consider a healthy increase only to learn that you'll be paying the increase and more for nonsubsidized benefits. One experience like that is usually worth ten discussions on attention to detail, and it happens all the time.

The largest benefit package is not necessarily the best because you probably can't use and don't need all of the benefits the organization offers. Only consider those you need and want. Many people are seduced by the wonderful color brochures on slick paper which companies have developed to sell the intrinsic value of their benefit plans. Be skeptical. These benefits may be provided as a substitute for money. Compare salaries very carefully. If the benefit package is excessive, that is, it's difficult to imagine anything anyone could need or want not covered, and the salary is competitive, where is the money coming from? In order to remain competitive in any market, one company can't offer a tremendously better deal than all of its competitors. If the company is, the money being funnelled into benefits is coming from somewhere. If it's able to be so lavish because it's far and away the most profitable company in the industry, so much the better. It may be salaries or it may mean that the company expects a much higher level of productivity with less support from its people. Half a person for every two jobs may be the rule rather than a person and a half for each job. Find out.

Get the Facts

Most personnel departments, once they know a manager is interested in hiring you, are anxious to explain all of the company's benefits. These people should be able to answer all questions or refer you. Don't consider this a perfunctory briefing. Take notes, mark up their brochures, treat it seriously. If you don't, you'll never be sure that you're truly getting more. Benefits in many places cost the organization about 25 to 45 percent of total salaries additional. If you're making $20,000 a year, the company is shelling out $5,000 to $9,000 additional to pay for the benefit package. That is nontaxable income to you if you need and want the benefits.

If there are benefits you wouldn't automatically get but which would be very useful, ask about them. There is no harm in trying to negotiate for an extra week's vacation in place of a life insurance policy. The cost to the company may be the same. Ask about tuition remission. You may be the only one who's been interested, and they may kick it in if they really want you. How about a company car or company-paid attendance at trade and professional meetings and conventions? How about some additional training that is job related? If you don't make up a shopping list, it's sure that no prospective boss will be able to read your mind and offer the right thing.

Our experience has been that the easiest trade-off has been vacation for life insurance in a very large company. The size of the insurable group can vary by a few people or even a certain percentage of total employees without affecting the overall rate the company must pay. What they pay yearly for term insurance on you may be less than your weekly salary plus remaining benefits. If you have family plan health insurance which is extremely comprehensive through your spouse's company, perhaps you can trade your company's policy for tuition remission or vacation. You may be surprised to know that most large organizations are self-insured. Blue Cross/Blue Shield and its competitors administer company programs and handle claims, but the company actually pays all of the medical bills plus an administration fee. That means the organization has a certain idea of how much it is likely to pay for you. If you ask for a rechanneling of that money, you may be surprised by an acceptance.

If you've done your homework, you are armed to negotiate. Otherwise you really have no leverage because, as usual, the organization has total knowledge, and you have zero. The more important it is to you to make trade-offs, the more homework you'll need to do. Once you have your numbers in place and verified, you're ready to build a game plan.

4

Where Are You Now?

In the old days—20 or so years ago—job security was believed to be the rule in employment, not the exception. A 1961 college graduate going through placement interviews was as likely to inquire about pensions and benefits as his or her opportunities to advance. It was assumed that, outside the glamour industries, that is, the print and broadcast media, publishing, advertising, show business, etc., you would probably be with one company for quite a long time. The most popular advice to women in the 1960s was, "Get your degree in teaching, you'll always have a job." Men were told to get degrees in management for the same reason. The emphasis in both cases was security. (The fact that teaching has turned out to be the least secure of professions in the 1970s and 1980s has been an embarrassment to vocational counselors.) Job hopping was something people with personality problems did.

Search firms did not starve but there were considerably fewer in 1961 than exist in 1981. The idea of being loyal to an organization and the organization being loyal in return was quite popular. Some companies even had official written policies to that effect. This was very strong in nonprofit organizations which liked to think of themselves as extended "families." If you went to work for a university in a nonfaculty position at 22 or 23, it was likely you would receive a gold watch on your retirement if you performed reasonably well.

Myth of Job Security

Job security was never as absolute as it seemed in the mythology, but it was widespread. Almost everyone in an established organization could point out a Hilda or Bob who had been there his or her whole career. On the worker's side, it was assumed that once you proved yourself, you had a reasonable expectation of job security. You would never be fired for whim—just for cause, for example, not doing the job, insubordination, absences, etc. There seemed to be an adherence to a mutually understood standard of fairness.

Social service agencies and universities; owner/founder businesses with owners who religiously stuck by employees; even the various branches of government subject to civil service did fire people occasionally. They did this discreetly and only in cases so blatant that no one could possibly pity the axed. The process of firing only the people who by consensus were incompetent (and not all of those) was very important. If you were incompetent, but had personal problems, marital or alcohol problems or simply needed the job, you might be spared. Most top management people recognized job security as a tremendously emotional issue. They packaged firings to make it seem that the fired one had practically begged to be fired. Unions certainly have always recognized the tremendously emotional nature of firing. Layoffs based on seniority and elaborate grievance procedures were and are one way of defusing this.

End of an Era

Something began to erode that philosophy in the 1970s. We talked to about 25 top management people in different size organizations about this change in both philosophy and business climate. They offered two ideas:

1. *Inflation seriously eroded many organizations' abilities to carry every employee through a business recession.* Not only production workers were cut in the 1974–1975 recession but many professional, technical, and middle managers as well. There was no fat and no compensating growth in the 1970s for many companies. If a business's survival was at stake, speed in minimizing the surplus was more important than a veneer of fairness.

2. *Worker attitudes changed.* Younger workers made no bones about their lack of commitment to the organization as an organization. Management bemoaned this lack of loyalty at first and then reciprocated when it found that the new generation of workers did not appear to appreciate job security or to see it as a benefit. As one manager said, "We kept talking about job security until we realized that most of our younger workers didn't care. They were fast trackers and wanted no guilt when they moved on."

The Inflation Effect

As productivity declined in the 1970s and inflation began to roar out of control, top management everywhere began to examine the idea of lifetime employment. As Americans look at the Japanese model, where people work for companies for a lifetime with no fear of firing, they are really looking at a different culture and vastly different set of expectations. Job security in America has become a formidable problem with scarce, expensive money, shifting values, and no guarantees that any company has an absolutely secure future.

For instance, Exxon, which has replaced General Motors as the largest industrial on the *Fortune* "500" list derives a great deal of profit from oil. Suppose a mad scientist in Wayward, Iowa, invents a synthetic fuel and refuses to cut Exxon—or any of the oil companies—in. He finds he can sell a perfectly acceptable gasoline substitute for 25 cents a gallon and still make millions. Will Exxon and Standard be forced to lay off employees? Will they do so despite all of the years of service the faithful have given? They will scramble to keep the organization alive until they find, buy, or barter for a competitive synthetic fuel. No one, including a great many employees, would expect them to do otherwise.

Management consultants are grappling with the need to lay off employees versus the poor public relations such actions result in. Instead of trying to prevent layoffs, many have begun advising clients on the best ways to soften the communications problems that result. This is an acknowledgment of a new attitude in a very different economic climate.

It is not remotely possible that all of the people laid off permanently by the auto manufacturers had performance problems. A great many were hard working, loyal, productive, and eager to remain on the payroll. They did not long to be standing in some state's unemployment office explaining what they'd been doing for the past 10 or 20 years. The people who worked 10 years for Chrysler or Ford may have loved their jobs and been very good at them. They had absolutely no control over their economic destinies, unless they were working strictly as a lark. The lark group is so tiny we needn't give them a thought.

The point is that the kind of job security people now in their sixties remember with such nostalgia as a postdepression phenomenon does not exist anymore except in very special circumstances: when you own the business, for instance. As the owner, as long as the business operates, you will have a job. Job security probably never existed as broadly as old-timers would suggest. Outside the federal government, schools and universities with tenure systems, and a few special companies, job security was more a cherished myth than an absolute fact.

Job security depended on an overall economic climate and a company climate that did not have frequent long-term upheavals. It meant organizations had reserves, usually quite fat, that could be used during short-term lean times: a two-year recession for example. Even so, job security was generally confined to two groups: Those at the lowest end of the pay scale, for example, clerks and secretaries, other service workers, or those nearing retirement. Once the company had exploited a woman for 20 years, paying her as little as possible, it was hardly a strain to keep her on until retirement. This was especially true when to have fired her would have caused severe dislocations among all of the people she knew in the organization.

As secretaries began to want greater upward mobility, the job security issue was raised by management as a benefit of employment. It was a fairly cheap way to buy a reputation among employees for loyalty and "heart." What of the employee nearing retirement who had decided to take early retirement while still on the job? If the employee has been very productive over the years and he or she could be forced out at 55, why not keep him or her on? Why get everybody rattled, cast a boss as a heavy, for so little gain? That was thinking fat.

Some companies never provided job security. The more pressure there was to increase profits every year, the more management prided itself on running lean, the less likely anyone in that organization was to have, or see him or herself as having, genuine job security. These companies have not changed their philosophies a bit. They are doing what they always have. Primarily these include the glamour industries where most people expect some periods of unemployment over a career.

Changing Values

Sometime after the Vietnam war, a new generation of workers arrived on the scene. They were interested in an entirely different career agenda. Job security was nothing to them compared to the idea of the fast track. As one man, 35, said, "I

am interested in only one thing: I want to run in the fast lane."
This new generation did not see company loyalty as a two-way
street. They never expressed this view to top management be-
case that would not have been politic. They simply never
bought in. Their strategy was that if management did not recognize their sterling qualities quickly and react accordingly,
they would move on. Search firms began to do better business
and hundreds more formed up and hustled to the action.

That wave of fast trackers ran into a problem that they had
not anticipated nor studied in their MBA case study courses.
The economy was not growing, and there was not as much upward thrust. The model of the 1960s could not be used at all.
The Vietnam war provided a lot of jobs, directly and in-
directly, that were no longer there. Only the people in the
"right" careers were doing relatively well. (The problem with
the "right" careers was that they changed from year to year.)
Some very hard working fast trackers had to make job changes
in the late 1970s for opportunity rather than cash. This was
disturbing to them and not the way things should be. Then
they met massive layoffs, reorganizations, a ruthless pruning of
unprofitable divisions, managements stingy with severance
pay—if they provided it at all—and takeovers. Apparently job
security was far more dead than anyone had realized.

All of this was happening not just in the *Fortune* "500" but
in much smaller businesses as well. It happened to those the
Wall Street Journal rarely covers. With fewer reserves, less
friendly bankers, and sometimes less sophisticated management, smaller companies were even more vulnerable to laying
off people with insufficient warning. However, as one woman
pointed out, for her, two years notice would hardly be sufficient as she disliked job hunting intensely.

The New Security

Job security as an idea or even an ideal has not died, but it is
very different from the sort of thing earlier generations ex-

pected, understood, and actually revered. The new job security is not security *with* a particular company, but security *from* dependence on any company.

The new job security acknowledges that no company can guarantee anyone, under contract or hired on a handshake, total job security. In the 1980s the very concept may disappear. It will not disappear because no organization can guarantee individual security, but because there is no need to. It is no longer a selling point. In a double-digit inflation, the largest group of workers think they want cash, not job security.

There are plenty of skilled, educated people who can be hired to do jobs, particularly given the tremendous numbers of baby boomers between 23 and 35, so that retaining every competent worker simply is not worth the loss of flexibility. Despite the cries of companies that they want employee loyalty, that they want to insure "home grown" top management, the price of doing so is simply too high. The need to buy the kind of talent that is needed at a particular time, with the ability to throw the person back into the pool if he or she becomes burdensome or no longer productive, is greater than the need for absolute loyalty. Indeed, many managers prefer the employee who sees him- or herself as an independent contractor. They are so much easier to lay off. There is no emotional content in the relationship. It is guilt-free on both sides.

This new breed of employee understands the new job security. Instead of concentrating on trying to find a safe berth in a company, that individual looks for a particular kind of manager, one who will help him or her along without extracting promises of forever or using a forever timetable or "down the line" for promotions and raises. This new employee worships movement above security, sometimes as much as or even more than money.

Moving into the 1980s, some of the fast trackers who have been burned by too much upheaval, especially those who did not survive the 1979–1980 recession layoffs, are asking themselves how to reinstitute or locate the old-fashioned job security. (Not every baby boomer has bought into this mind-set. The group that searches for the old-style security is probably no more than 20 percent of the market.) In an increasingly conservative business climate, this 20 percent is willing to forsake the fast lane for a relief from anxiety about their own economic status. Some are even considering working for the government, something few could have imagined as eager college or MBA graduates.

For many baby boomers, movement is a substitute for upward mobility. It feels like progress, it is less boring than waiting, and it is not so damaging to the ego.

As one woman said, "Of course I'm kidding myself. I know I'm not advancing as quickly as I should, but at least I'm not stagnating."

For most, however, the new job security, simply put, must be self-generated. It is in part a lifestyle security. In order to function well in a very uncertain economy, the individual sees him- or herself as solely responsible for providing economic security. In other words, the person is self-managed in a whole new way.

Rather than accept the limitation of picking jobs on the basis of whether or not the company's long-term prospects are better than average in the general economic climate, the self-managed individual chooses each job as someone would pick up a piece of a jigsaw puzzle. This individual is never as concerned with the longevity of a particular job so much as its place in the puzzle he or she is putting together.

The puzzle idea results from a heightened interest in career planning, plus a recognition of the new reality.

The bottom line in such a strategy is economic. It depends on a flexible standard of living, something that most people would not have considered five years ago. If you remember five years ago, people set consumption goals rather than career goals. "As soon as I get promoted we'll leave the apartment and buy a condominium. We'll live there three years and, if we both get big raises, we'll sell that and get a house." The emphasis was on moving up at regular intervals. The philosophy was, "Look, we should do these things because we can afford it and everyone we know is doing it."

"I must live downtown because that's where all of the other singles are, and I'll have to pay a premium for the privilege." Sometimes called "keeping up with the Joneses," this philosophy is on the ropes with the baby boomers. It allows for no flexibility. It stands for being locked in, economically and emotionally. In order to provide one's own job security, one must be able to live below, sometimes significantly below his or her standard of living. If he or she lives above it, there is no room to move around. Hence, there can be no risk taking. To take a risk requires some cushion which the financially overextended do not have. As so many people who work for nonprofit organizations say by their longevity with those organizations, "Half a loaf that's steady is much better than a whole loaf or more I'd have to worry about."

You, on the other hand, must have at least a somewhat different philosophy or you would not be reading this book. If you're really thinking about how to beat inflation or at least be less vulnerable economically, you are not entirely adverse to thinking about things in a new way. Begin by looking at the way you live. Could you lower your standard of living? What lifestyle flexibility to you have?

What are your lifestyle goals?

Before you run for your family budget book to calculate net worth, ask yourself about your lifestyle. What is your lifestyle? It is how you choose to live. It is as much an expression of your personal philosophy as the corporation's policies are of its philosophy.

One of the things that makes this discussion difficult is that most of us have learned to block our real responses. We have learned to do what sells. Therefore, whatever lifestyle is chic, many adopt it. While this is useful in many instances, it is not good here.

If you are not constantly improving or embellishing your

lifestyle, do you see yourself falling behind? Lots of people do. They feel that if they are not spending more, whether it is to buy things, vacations, education, whatever, they are losing out. On the other hand, a large group is learning to do things differently. Witness the decline in brand loyalty as many people rush to buy generic brands at the supermarket. The fast track philosophy uses money as a benchmark. If you are to have the luxury of job choice, if you are to make you salary match or exceed inflation, if you are to provide your own job security, you will have to reorient your thinking.

What are your salary goals?

If your goal is to make as much money as you possibly can, that is called greed, not goal setting. You will have to refine your thinking on this issue as well as be much more specific. There are a number of goals compatible with some self-provided security.

• *You can maximize your earning potential from age 22 to 30 by changing jobs every year to 18 months.* If you are in a glamour industry, this may be a good strategy because starting salaries are abysmally low. It is also useful for anyone affected with salary compression. (Compression means that starting salaries rise much faster than do those of people who stay year after year.) It allows you to get much larger raises than you could expect at annual reviews. The average annual salary increase ranged from 7 to 12 percent in the late 1970s counting merit increases. A move from company to company or a promotion was worth 10 to 20 percent. Since you are under 30, you will not have as many problems with the "job hopper" label as someone doing this in his or her 30s or 40s. It can mean 30 percent more cash over a 3-year period.

• *You can spend the first few years of your career, the time under 30, building a solid foundation of experience with an organization that pays off in training, not dollars.* At 30 you can begin a judicious series of changes over the next 10 to 15 years which put you in a top spot by the age of 45. You will need to change every two to three years, but you will be constantly on the lookout for opportunities. Then you will perch in a suitable company until you vest in its retirement program, probably ten years. Then you may move again if another opportunity comes along. If you have an IRA and have done some financial planning, you may not care about vesting.

• *You can go to work for the largest growing firm you can find that values the skills you have to offer and concentrate on moving around internally both up the ladder and from ladder to ladder.* This means you are prepared and committed to retooling periodically. You are going to be constantly job hunting just as with the first option, but all under one umbrella. You will need highly developed political skills and concentration.

You can use a combination or variation of any of these. The important idea is that you will have some goals and a plan. If you are 40 now, what has been your path even if you did not consciously think about it at the time? The boat has not left yet. There is still plenty of time to get on board. The important thing is that your plan must match your philosophy and be designed to meet your salary goals.

Anteing Up

Obviously, all of this depends on your being able to take some risks. A risk is simply the chance that something will, or will not, happen. There is a knowable risk that if you take up sky diving it will shorten your life. There is a knowable risk that when you cross the street with the walk light you will not make it to the other side. It is very small in that case, but it is there and it is measurable.

How much risk are you comfortable with? Can you work effectively in a situation in which your job may be on the line every day but you are earning top dollar, possibly significantly above market? What is your comfort and/or stress level? Would you happily settle for 20 percent less salary to buy less anxiety about what you will do or where you will be tomorrow? Keep in mind that these choices are not absolute, or one-time-only. To repeat: there is no such thing as absolute job security. You keep making or reaffirming a choice every day. You are not going to be secure in the 1980s as far as any economist, far left to far right, can see. Therefore, you are going to be some kind of risk taker. The question is, what kind?

The amount or risk you can comfortably handle will depend on what you see as your backup system. If you are blessed with a wealthy, generous parent, your situation is different from someone with no savings who is getting aggressive collection calls from MasterCard and Visa. The old rule that everyone needs at least six months' salary in cash savings to provide some kind of security in case of unemployment is too strict. What you may need is two months' salary in a money market fund and some stock which could be sold, preferably at a profit, on short notice. Forget conventional savings accounts unless something dramatic happens to interest rates very soon.

Unless you have this kind of backup, you may scare yourself to death if you try any of the more risky strategies in this book, especially if you have dependents. Our experience has been that higher risk strategies require a kind of confidence that someone scared to death of economic disaster cannot quite muster.

By now you have no doubt discovered that wresting more money from your present employer or a new one is not going to be easy. Even the ability to try depends on preplanning and a careful consideration of your lifestyle and financial resources. If you have never given a thought to a written budget or a financial plan, now is the time. Get help from someone who knows about financial planning to help you develop a plan you can live with.

The best source for setting up a budget, doing tax planning, and getting continuous information is a certified public accountant who works primarily with individuals. You are not too poor or too strapped to forgo this service. Begin asking your friends who they use or who they have heard is good. The rule of thumb in seeking financial advice is this: Never trust financial planning to someone who is trying to sell you something. Take advice from someone who makes his or her money selling *advice,* not as a percentage of what you buy. Someone who gives advice but sells insurance on the side is not going to give you the quality advice you need. Get references on the person you propose to work with before you even call for an exploratory appointment.

Analyzing Lifestyle

What about your lifestyle? There are not many lifestyle analysts around who will help. Here are the issues you want to consider in deciding how flexible your style is.

• *Where do you live and why did you pick that location?* Is it the only place you see yourself? What percentage of your *net* (after tax) income goes for housing? Consider what your location is intended to say about you. Are you concerned with living in the right sort of place? (Be honest. There is no right or wrong answer and nothing to be gained by kidding yourself.) If you are spending more than 25 percent of your pretax income on housing, you have a problem. You are less flexible and less able to take risks than someone spending 25 percent of after tax dollars. Do not forget that you are being forced into a higher tax bracket with every yearly raise and certainly if your income goes up significantly as you change jobs.

• *How fashionable are you?* Do you get rid of last year's clothes when they are judged unfashionable or simply because they are last year's? How often do you redecorate? What percentage of your income is spent on fad and fashion together? If this figure approaches 30 percent after taxes, again you are less flexible, especially if any of this amount is financed with revolving charges. You would have to include the 18 to 24 percent interest you pay as part of this category.

• *What percentage of your income goes for convenience?* Do you take cabs home if it is too much trouble to wait for a bus or subway? Do you drive in spite of public transportation because it is more comfortable or more convenient? Do you eat in restaurants because cooking takes too long? Who picks up and delivers and how often? If this category exceeds 20 percent pretax, it is very high.

• *How do you feel about vacations?* Are you interested in places you have never been primarily so you can say that you have seen or done them? Do you buy package tours? Do you return to the same place year after year?

• *How often do you make a change?* If you enjoy change for its own sake, if nothing is permanent, you are potentially flexible enough to make major lifestyle changes. This might also be called a sense of adventure.

• *On a continuum from adventurous to conventional, where would you put yourself?* This is another way of thinking about risk taking. If new ideas are at least worth thinking about just because they are new, you can make changes more easily. If you have a wait-and-see attitude, you are probably more conventional. Keep in mind we are talking about receptivity to new *ideas* not your fashion/fad consciousness level.

Your answers should reflect your gut feelings. If you spend more than 70 percent of your income on housing, fashion, and convenience items, your lifestyle if relatively inflexible. You are locked in financially. That does not mean you could not change. You may not have seen any reason to do so until now.

Do you want to change? You do not necessarily have to. There are ways that you can work around your lifestyle choices. Still, you need to know all the options because some are necessarily easier than others. By casting yourself in concrete financially, you forego some options and limit your ability to respond to or initiate change. In the next chapter you will be building your game plan. It is important to know what you have got to work with.

Options are trade-offs. If you are going to operate from a no risk position, your options are fewer. You cannot do the same sorts of things someone with more flexibility can do. The classic example of the trade-off is the man whose wife works at home taking care of two children under five. He is every company's ideal employee because he is relatively less able to move. He is trading the luxury of a stay-at-home wife for the greater cash and flexibility of two incomes. He needs that paycheck and will put up with more to keep it because of this choice. Contrast that with the single man who is only responsible for a sheep dog and keeping his room clean enough to suit his mother. If he wants to move the stakes are low. He can forego something this year for a higher return next year as he may not have to give up much at all.

What if inflation subsides or is reduced to a 5 to 7 percent level? Will this make any difference in your plans? While the most optimistic economist President Reagan has employed does not really forecast this in the predictable future, it would hardly be good planning to discount it entirely. Let us suppose that inflation does subside to 5 percent a year. In the 1960s there were periods like this and raises in some organizations did exceed the rate of inflation. Your problem, however, is one of worst case planning. In the best of circumstances you can relax a bit, but never completely. If you relax too much, or prematurely, you will find yourself having to play catch up.

You can always elect to settle in somewhere and work only within one organization. Nothing commits you to the life of a career nomad. If interests or priorities change and you have maintained your lifestyle flexibility, you can decide to work for an organization that seems to maximize both security and salary. The key to maintaining your options will always be lifestyle flexibility. If you can move to a lower or higher spending level quickly, you can take risks.

One of the principal methods used to secure your ability to move at will is contacts. At 25, 200 contacts will usually produce 10 live job opportunities to investigate. At 45, it takes 600

contacts for 10 live opportunities. This reflects the age discrimination that exists as well as much tougher standards for people
who will probably stay until retirement or beyond.

There are a number of questions you will need to ask yourself as you prepare to develop a strategy for getting more as
well as learn to negotiate once you have a plan.

• *What is your comfort level?* Do you have a bone-deep need
not to take risks and to get on with your life separate from your
economic/career life? If work and money are not central to
your self-esteem, there is no need for you to adopt the most
extreme strategy proposed here. You are not a candidate for
job hopping, early or late. Your attention will probably be better spent on financial planning and keeping yourself in the political favor of those who have power over your career. You
may choose to make fewer changes and less risky ones. You
may choose the large, steadily prosperous firm over the higher
payout of a higher risk, smaller place.

If risk does not make you uncomfortable, you can try virtually any of the strategies proposed in the next few chapters.
You must always keep in mind that you could suffer a temporary setback or be unemployed for a short period. You will
also have to work harder not just at your job, but at the fairly
constant job hunting needed to keep up contacts and be prepared to jump whenever it is advantageous. Truly your work
will never be done. Your trade-off will be time for money and
lots of time in the beginning. Once you reach a maintenance
level, it will be easier for you to keep up what you have built.

• *What kind of help will you need to develop your game plan?*
How much time will it take to locate such help? Our experience
has been that the planning process for a three-year plan will
take about 40 hours divided however best suits you. It is not a
one-afternoon or one-evening proposition. If you decide to get
professional help, you will need, in addition to an accountant,
some help from a career planner. There are any number of
one-day seminars you can attend in most communities. The
problem is they are not offered every day so there may be a

time lag. These have multiplied since the early 1970s so that many community colleges actually have full-time staff whose only function is career planning with adults. These people bear no resemblance to the comic strip vocational counselor armed with tests and the *Occupational Outlook Handbook,* probably the most obsolete publication in America. Like the stopped watch which is always right twice a day, the OOH is right for the wrong reasons. If the information reflects the market it is because the pendulum has swung back the other way and made the information current. The OOH is elderly before it is published and that is what makes it worthless.

Expect to spend from $50 to $100 for a one-day career planning seminar. Beware the private organizations that charge upwards of $300 for a one-day seminar. You are buying frosting. The quality of the instructor should be checked with people who have been through a seminar with that instructor. Do not buy a pig in a poke.

• *If temporarily unemployed, what can you do to make money while putting together the game plan?* Temporary work for some kind of temporary agency remains the best option unless you have a friend who will let you freelance. It is good because there is no need to account for it specifically on resume or application blank. It can be lumped together under the name of the agency. It is also a good way to get into various companies to look around and see what you can absorb. Remember that if the organization has a job posting system, you will see what is posted, and it will be useful in your research. Yes, most office temporary agencies do hire males who can type. If you are male and you cannot type, why not?

• *Do you have all the education you will need for what you are trying to do?* If everybody in the organization has a bachelor's degree and you have none, what are your options? You can enroll in a program posthaste or you can target a company headed by a college or high school dropout. You will have a harder time scaling the wall of the organization which has traditionally recruited only college graduates. Sometimes these companies will hire those within sight of a B.A. The same is true with organizations heavy with MBA's or other kinds of masters.

Once you have got your analysis done, you are ready to build the game plan.

5

Learning to Negotiate
for Money

Have you ever read a magazine or newspaper article on job hunting, much less a book, that doesn't include at least one reference to salary negotiation? That's the standard phrase and every job hunter has heard it at least a hundred times. But what does it mean? If you haven't been trained in negotiation, the tension of the moment coupled with your own sense of powerlessness and desperate desire for the job may undo you. Instead of planning and preparing to negotiate you find yourself praying that whatever you're offered will be something you can live with. Anything to get the process over with and get on with life.

Whether you're a prospective employee or just going in for an annual salary review, the conversation sometimes tends to be perfunctory. The boss says, "How does X percent sound?" You say, "Fine," and that's the end. This is not negotiating. This isn't even a discussion. Unless you learn to say more than, "Fine," your salary will always be much smaller than it needs to be. We haven't spent four chapters preparing to negotiate to agree to a first offer without so much as a whimper.

You've got to remember that this kind of negotiation does not depend on how much power you have or on your state of mind. It is a fact that most people, stupid or clever, really can't read minds. Therefore, your concern should be to make organization, facts, and strategy carry you, not rely on charisma, clever repartee, or good looks. Difficult as it may be to believe, the prospective boss does not have total power. You can say, "No, thank you." This forces him or her to begin again the ordeal of finding another hot prospect to bring along to the same final stage of negotiation where you are now. The power to say no is power. The only time the boss has significantly more or disproportionate power is when you've already told him or her that this is the only job in the world for you, and if you care about your career at all you won't have done this. Most bosses don't assume that a prospect has already made up his or her mind before hearing the offer. They think that looking interested and eager is *your* game. They know they are buying a service, your labor. As with every other service, they expect some give on both sides.

Setting the Stage

Imagine that you are in the final stages of negotiating for a new job. You and the prospective boss are pleased with each other and think that you can work together. You've talked about benefits, pension plans, working conditions, most of the nitty gritty except starting salary. You've done your homework and know what market is and what your salary range is. You want between $22,000 and $25,000 to take the job. Finally, the opening question comes. The prospective employer says, "Our last year was not as profitable as we expected. In fact, we had a hiring freeze for six months. I probably shouldn't be hiring anyone at all but we're really shorthanded. This job is a tremendous opportunity for someone who's looking for challenge and the opportunity to grow. Of course, it's not a place to get rich quickly." There's a pause. Then, looking you directly in the eye, the boss asks, "What salary range did you have in mind?"

You would need ironclad poise not to hesitate at least a split second, reevaluating what you were going to ask for, before you named your figure. You might be afraid to stick with your original decision. What if you don't get the job and you really want it? What if there are five other candidates all of whom named a much lower figure or who will come down on the figure they named? What if this is your only live prospect and you've been looking six months?

What the prospect has done, of course, is a classic opener of win/lose negotiating. Win/lose or Soviet-style negotiating means that if I win you lose. He or she prefaced the request for an opening bid from you with a statement that is designed to get you to reduce the amount you'll name. He or she has done this despite the fact that the company's troubled history isn't particularly attractive.

Take the opposite view. It could be argued that the company's less prosperous past would cause you to raise, not lower, the salary range you will suggest. After all, if the organization is on the ropes you're taking a higher risk by going to work there and risk must be paid for. The employer is probably not even considering that reaction. He or she assumes that if the plight of the company is thrown on the table you may name a lower figure, saving the trouble of negotiating back and forth until you reach a mutually agreeable figure. The whole opening ploy is designed to soften you up. This is used a great deal in nonprofit organizations. The more worthy the cause the organization exists for, the more likely it will be to try to get prospective employees to take satisfaction instead of cash. Some people have uncharitably referred to this as taking advantage of people—especially the young and/or desperate.

Unfortunately, most people think that whatever the employer offers, regardless of the situation, that offer is the first and final one. It's either too intimidating or too difficult to make a counter offer, especially if you'd really like the job, the raise, or the promotion. Yet, this is the one opportunity most people have to negotiate. It's even expected if not relished by the other side. Unless you're prepared to overcome a natural reluctance to make counter offers, your options are not just limited, they are nonexistent.

What Is Negotiation?

Negotiation is barter. It goes on at every flea market, garage sale, auction, even in some retail stores as well as between employees and employers. Most people who'd never dream of buying something from an antique dealer without making a counter offer are struck dumb by the prospect of making a counter offer to a boss or prospect. The process that makes a wiley bargainer at a flea market is the same that makes a successful negotiator anywhere.

Suppose you are at a flea market and you see an antique camera that you would love to have. Before you can talk to the dealer you have to know three things. (1) How much is the camera actually worth? How much could you buy it for somewhere else? (2) How much are you willing or able to pay? (3) How much is the dealer likely to take? Where should you begin your bidding?

The very same things must be discovered in an employment situation. There is no difference. You are no more a victim in the employee/employer negotiation than you are in the flea market. Remember that even in a recession there are a number of job opportunities for the enterprising searcher. If this boss refuses to negotiate you will find others more willing. If you insist on what you want at any price, in life or in a flea market, you'll pay much, much more. One of the things that makes many flea market dealers more ethical to deal with than employers is that if you appear not to know the game, they will say something like, "There is a little give in the price," or "I could take a little less." This signals you to make a counter offer. If the flea market dealer doesn't give you this help you may never do business with him or her again once you learn the game. Unfortunately this option rarely exists with employers.

In order to bargain with an employer or prospective employer you need to know the same three things. (1) How much is the job actually worth? What is the market rate? This is the material covered in Chapter Three. (2) How much are you willing to take for your services? What are you worth? You will need to know what you're willing to give up financially and in other ways to get the job. (3) What kinds of compromises is the boss likely to make? What are his or her hot buttons? How do you answer the boss to keep the bidding open and to secure your objectives?

Back to your negotiations. You are now faced with sizing up the boss' probable reaction to your request for $22,000 to $25,000. What if the boss is absolutely horrified by such a range and rejects it out of hand. What will you say? You need a strategy for starting and keeping negotiations on track as well as countering opposition.

In negotiating, a successful strategy always begins with a consideration of what's at stake for both sides. The easiest way to see how this works is to construct a negotiating grid.

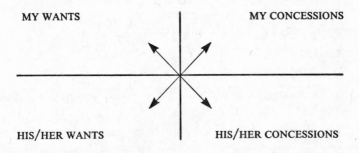

MY WANTS | MY CONCESSIONS

HIS/HER WANTS | HIS/HER CONCESSIONS

You will know what you want from the job because you have been talking about that right along. You also know what you need to secure in order to do a good job, or you should know. If you need an office with a door because cubicles cause you to break out in paranoia you've got to put it on your list. This is your prinicipal opportunity to start the job on the right foot. If you think that negotiating before you are hired is tough, think how much tougher it will be when you try to re-negotiate after you're on board. You have no leverage at all then. Ordinarily you'd have to wait until the first review and that could be 12 to 18 months away.

You will not have as clear an idea of what the prospective employer wants but you will have some idea if you've listened carefully, asked the right questions, and checked the boss out with former employees. As you have been talking with this person you've gotten a fair idea of what his or her values are. You know this from what's been emphasized in both questions and conversation. Some of this raw material will require a little thought. This is essential if you're to negotiate effectively and certainly if your grid is to be comprehensive.

Your Wants

Let's look at your wants first. Your list might look something like this, written in order of declining importance.

1. $22,000 minimum salary
2. Three weeks paid vacation
3. Full health and life insurance coverage
4. $1,500 in tuition benefits toward the MBA
5. Mentor
6. Company-paid attendance at two industry meetings a year
7. Company-paid membership in two industry associations
8. First salary review in 12, not 18 months
9. Secretary not shared with anyone else
10. Expense account, company-paid American Express card
11. Opportunity to become visible in the organization
12. Opportunity to interact with other departments

You have included both economic and noneconomic issues. This is very important because you will almost always negotiate both intertwined as you move toward a final offer and acceptance or rejection.

Your Concessions

Now you must list your concessions. Most people find they have many fewer concessions than they have demands—an entirely human circumstance. Still, you need to have at least two major things and a few minor ones to throw into the pot. The things you're willing to concede need not all match your list of wants. It's likely some of them will match the prospect's wants.

After considerable thought you decide on the following concessions.

1. Two weeks paid vacation with the option of unpaid leave for the third week
2. $1,000 in tuition benefits toward the MBA instead of $1,500
3. Sharing a secretary
4. No expense account for the first six months
5. Low profile for the first year

Would starting salary be nonnegotiable or is it possible you'll take less under certain circumstances? You now look at linked concessions. If you were to accept $21,000, then the first salary review would have to be at the end of six months. You are willing to start lower when an early review, and presumably raise, is guaranteed. Guaranteed usually means that the boss gives you a letter of intent spelling out the details of the company's offer. This may or may not be legally enforceable, but it would be difficult for the company not to honor it if you have a signed letter.

You might link the $21,000 salary to $2,500 in tuition remission. This would more than make up for the loss of the $1,000 in salary the first year because the $2,500 is not taxable. (The

IRS would like to tax tuition benefits but hasn't been able to so far.) Below $21,000 you may have trouble finding trade-offs you'd accept as that approaches what you earned before.

Boss's Wants

What does the boss want? You review mentally your conversations with the prospective boss and other employees in the past. His or her tentative want list may look like this.

1. Hardest working employee I can get at the lowest price
2. More productive—creates a "surplus"
3. Steady, dependable worker who'll stay at least three years
4. Will follow my orders and do it my way
5. Someone who'll work on my team and support my career—loyal
6. Requiring little or no supervision and training. Lands on his/her feet and starts running
7. Class and style—not too many rough edges
8. Not too demanding
9. Not a threat to me, I'm getting tired of struggling and I want to enjoy the job more
10. I want to look good in front of my superiors

You cannot know at the time you're writing this which, if any of these wants, are on your prospect's want list. You must be prepared to probe during the time of your negotiation to see which are valid and in what order.

Boss's Concessions

Your prospect's concession list may be short or long. You don't know. What you do know is what he or she might concede or trade, that is, what it is *possible* for him or her to trade. You can't predict if he or she will. Basically this list might be as follows.

1. More money
2. More vacation. If the company is small enough so personnel is not powerful enough to prevent a manager making this commitment. (Many personnel departments aren't.)
3. Change of salary grade if you're one of a kind or one of a few of a kind
4. Change in first salary review date, making the first salary review date sooner or later
5. A starting salary above the midpoint
6. More visibility in the organization, actually pushing your career. This is most likely to happen when you are working for a boss who is not threatened by you or your ambition.
7. Mentoring either by a Godfather (making this happen) or an information mentor (explaining how the organization really works and where the power buttons are). Beware! Some people who have the power to mentor have no talent at teaching and nurturing, which is what mentoring requires.

How much a boss is willing to give will depend on two things. It will be about 60 percent how well you've sold him or her and 40 percent how closely you seem to meet what the boss had in mind. Never underestimate mindset as an important variable. People who have in mind a particular kind of person are often reluctant to try something else. They want the mental picture.

Back to your boss's opening statement. The suggestion has been made that the company wants to sell challenge and the opportunity to grow, not pay top dollar. It's been implied that the company can't pay too much, whatever that means in dollars.

Never disagree with the prospect especially since there is nothing to disagree with. Saying, "Of course I'm interested in growth and challenge, *but,*" will put off the employer. It's much better to say, "I'm sure that there is tremendous opportunity for growth and challenge here. I'm certainly interested in that. What I have in mind is a combination of elements with a financial package which includes a starting salary of $22,000 to $25,000." You do not repeat or counter the prospect's opening statement. Strictly speaking you haven't been *asked* to comment on that.

At this point you want to wait until the prospect reacts. If you rush on with the rest of your list, or begin to defend your numbers, you will obscure the major issue. After all, you put the starting salary first. That means it should be most important.

Here are some things to keep in mind during the negotiating session.

• *Don't rush.* The worst thing you can do in negotiating is to rush through the process. If you don't talk about what you want, step by step, letting the other side react to each proposal individually, you risk having some very important things lost or dealt with too lightly.

• *Don't be afraid of silence.* Don't jump in, while the prospect is thinking, and say something like, "Of course, if that's too much, I'd be willing to take $21,000 if it's coupled with an extra week's vacation." Let the prospect have a chance to think. You don't know what he or she is thinking until something is said. You're not learning a thing babbling on and on and confusing the issue. This also puts you at a serious disadvantage because the prospect sees you as desperate and therefore vulnerable. Finally it's unbusinesslike.

• *Don't offer any arguments.* You've been asked a question which you've answered. Wait to be asked why. The game goes more smoothly when you hit the ball over the net and wait for it to come back to you. If asked where you got the numbers, explain. "This is market right now in our area. I checked with (list the organizations you got your information from)." Don't be defensive and don't consider this an adversarial proceeding. Wouldn't you want to know where someone's numbers came from if they were selling you something?

• *You are engaged in win/win negotiations.* You're not trying to beat the prospective boss, with whom you expect to work comfortably, out of the last dime. You're trying to arrive at a mutually satisfactory arrangement that will allow both of you to feel that you made a good bargain. Compromise can't be an objective because that usually means each side gives up some things it wanted and takes some things it didn't want. If you are negotiating properly you'll both get a majority of what you wanted.

• *Answer each question thoroughly but without adding any extraneous material.* Don't start a sideshow. If you're talking about cash, don't bring up the pension plan at that time. The time to do linkages is if the negotiations deadlock.

Suppose that the boss agrees to a starting salary of $22,500 at his or her suggestion. Then, as you go down your list, it becomes clear that the major sticking point is something you hadn't anticipated. This particular boss absolutely despises trade and professional associations and particularly the ones you propose to have him or her pay for. This is low on your list so you can afford to concede the paid memberships and attendance. It would be a mistake, however, not to find out if the boss's opinion is so strong that even if *you* pay your own way, your attendance and participation will be held against you.

Again, this negotiating session is not just important for what you'll win but in helping you gauge what this person's attitudes on important work-related issues are likely to be once you're on board. You haven't agreed to work for this person yet, and if his or her views turn out to be too far from yours you may not.

Most of this would not have come out in your previous interviews because they have, by their nature, been very general. There has not been anything as specific as the issue of your membership in a particular organization, to trigger a specific reaction. Both of you have talked about what you'd do "in general," "ordinarily," or "most of the time." Listen carefully and make mental notes about the salient points. You have few other such opportunities for frank discussion before you're on board. Once you're working for this boss your conversations may be more political or packaged than frank.

If it's obvious that there is not going to be agreement at this time, go on with the rest of your list. Say, "Can we come back to this in a minute? I've got some other things I would like to talk about." This buys you some thinking time and also gives the boss a chance to rethink his or her position.

Even if some of the economic issues have already been discussed you will want to bring them up again to make sure that your starting salary didn't dislodge anything. This is important as the deal would be undone if there's a misunderstanding.

Suppose the rest of your list is agreed to. So far you haven't had to compromise or give up anything. Then, as you prepare to return to the trade association issue the prospective boss throws a curve. "This is all subject to approval by the personnel department, of course," he or she says. At this point the tendency is to ask whether personnel is likely to raise a stink about anything you've agreed on. Don't. Wait and let the boss offer more information.

If you say anything you're inviting him or her to suggest areas in which there could be problems. The temptation is to say, "I could take less," or "That's not as important to me as this." Many times the bringing of personnel into the conversation at this point is a negotiating ploy. It is the boss's attempt to establish personnel as a scapegoat in case he or she should have a change of heart. If you accept personnel as more powerful than the person you are negotiating with you buy the scapegoat argument. The important thing is to hold the boss for whom you'll work responsible for what he or she has promised.

If there's a change of heart it will be up to the boss to reopen negotiations with you. If you must make some response say, "I didn't realize that personnel could override the decisions of line managers." This implies that you know who is more powerful. If the manager begins to hedge and suggests that personnel can and will override any agreement he or she makes, you are negotiating with the wrong person. Unhappily you may not learn this until the final negotiations.

Other important points to keep in mind during this process are:

• *Don't make concessions out of fear.* If someone says something that seems to imply that you should back down, don't do so unless you are asked if you could change, take less, or forego that point entirely. Both sides are testing and this is part of the process.

• *Keep the discussion impersonal.* If both of you get excited, you are more likely to lose control of the process. Don't go for every ploy offered. Think before you respond. This doesn't have to be wrapped up in three minutes. What could be more important to you than what you are negotiating?

• *Don't keep beating a dead issue.* If you and the prospect deadlock on an issue and the discussion gets heated, suggest moving on and coming back to that point in a minute. It may be something you'll have to think about very hard before you agree to take the job, regardless of the rest of the package.

• *You can have a written out proposal which you share with the prospect or you can have one you refer to occasionally.* Explain this by saying that you've "made some notes so I won't forget anything."

• *Don't worry if you feel embarrassed.* That's natural. Money is still a taboo subject. You don't have serious money discussions every day. You can afford to keep yourself under tight control for what may be an hour at the most.

• *Ask the prospect if there are any other things he or she is interested in.* You may be surprised as what your setting up the session in this way may have unleashed. The prospect may begin to add to his or her list of wants and provide more opportunity to agree or not. This is good because it's always better to know what someone wants in as much detail as possible.

• *If you agree on things which weren't in the written job description you may need to suggest that this document be rewritten.* If it's not redone you may have a problem once on the job. Memory is a matter of convenience and self-interest.

After both of you have said all you have to say, ask when he or she would like a decision. It's important to find out if the prospect will put what you've agreed to in writing or if he or she would prefer you did. The point is that someone should put what was agreed on in writing. Volunteer to do a summary and send it to him or her. This is not an employment contract. If the prospect writes it, it is a letter of intent and if you do it's a reverse letter of intent. Employment contracts need lawyers. Unless there is a very good reason to get a contract, it may be better for you to work on a handshake.

• *At the end of the session offer to write a summary of what was agreed.* The object is to get all that was agreed to in writing as quickly as possible. It's not too important which of you does this although it's to your advantage to do it. That way, you make sure that your version becomes the official version. However, if the boss says that he or she will put everything in writing, agree. You won't be able to make a decision or even predict your decision until you see the written form of the negotiations. This should be made clear. Some prospects think that an oral agreement should be enough. These are people who sometimes talk about "flexibility" and "trust." The only flexible money is that printed by the government. Get it in writing. This is not a matter of trust, it's a matter of good business practice.

Occasionally you meet with someone who refused to put anything you have discussed in writing. You want the job but you also want some kind of definite agreement. After you leave this session you will need to send the prospect a written summary asking whether this version is as he or she remembers. Say, in the last paragraph, "If I don't hear from you within forty-eight hours I'll assume that we're in agreement." The copy you send the prospect has a 90 percent chance of ending up in your personnel file. Then if any question comes up about any of the terms, you have both your original and the office copy in your personnel file.

A boss who says positively he or she can't or won't be bound by anything the two of you have negotiated but that he or she will try, is presenting a calculated risk. How much do you want the job? That's always the bottom line in these situations. Almost everyone under 30 has had at least one negotiating situation that ended this way. Most of them decided they'd take a chance. All that we talked to regretted it.

The enraged helplessness which results from a situation in which promises are not kept or deliberately overturned takes quite awhile to go away. Of course there are no guarantees. You are laying a base that hopefully will convince the prospect that you intend the relationship to be more professional than personal. Don't ever trust the boss who says, "Trust me." Trust should be possible because the person you're dealing with has integrity. Unfortunately too many bosses think integrity has less use in business than expediency. If you've done your homework, you won't be dealing with a totally unknown quantity. Most everyone has some former employers who can give them references. You should have found these people before you got this far into the process.

• *Don't agree to take the job at the end of the negotiating session.* Always set a time in which you will respond to the offer. If you agree to take the job before you've seen anything in writing, what will you do if the version you do see is nothing like your memory of the session? Or worse still, no written version materializes? Anywhere from three days to two weeks is appropriate as a period for you to think over the offer. You may have other prospects on the horizon you want to explore further. If you went into the session determined to get the job at any price, it's still poor business to accept until all the terms have been committed in writing. You can hint that you think the job sounds ideal but don't commit yourself until you've had a chance to think the offer over. You may think of ten questions you need answered. Once you agree to take the job the terms are set.

• *If you are very disappointed in the final offer but you need a job desperately you may decide to take the job but keep looking.* This has some ethical problems but no more than the boss who hires people during a reorganization or merger. However, if the offer was below market and the arrangements are substandard you needn't feel too bad. Turnover is a way of life in this situation. Unless you have the proverbial rich uncle you'll have to look out for your own interests.

Keep in mind that you can't be ruined by one poor choice. The younger you are, the less damage your career sustains. You may have to learn some of the fine points about negotiating by trial and error. However, you can be armed against some of the more common games prospects play. See Chapter 6.

6

Employer Tricks, Ripoffs, and Games

Employers are an inventive lot. Used to dealing with wiley sales people, their own superiors, and ego-invested in their own power, they like to win. To many, negotiating with either an employee or a prospective employee is a win/lose situation. They will use many different techniques to get employees and prospective employees to agree to what they want or think is "reasonable." One of the joys, loosely speaking, of interviewing is the opportunity to observe the Byzantine methods employers will use to get a very good employee on board at a very minimal price. After all, the bottom line must be served and fairness rarely does that as well as games. Because you need to be prepared to counter these ploys in a way that is polite, businesslike, but *firm,* we have included the most frequently used ones with a strategy for you. Before we get to those, there are seven principles to keep in mind.

• *Tone of voice and body language are vital.* Like a mouse eyed hungrily by a cat, you are being looked over and evaluated. If you seem calm and confident, this makes an impression on the other side. An obviously nervous, desperate negotiator is the perfect victim.

• *Do not overreact and do not personalize.* Remember that the person across the table, whether an employer you have worked for for several years or someone you have met twice, does not really know you and your vulnerabilities. Only your family and friends know you well enough to hit you where it really hurts. If this person does score a hit he or she has made a lucky shot or a shrewd guess. He or she is trying different plays. What he or she is doing reflects what has been effective in the past, not on a personal knowledge of you and what makes you cringe. In other words, do not react to or regard these discussions as personal. Most people, particularly your superiors, see you only in outline. They neither know nor care what you as a human being are really like. Protect your psyche by reminding yourself at least fifty times a day that because something *seems* personal does not make it personal.

• *Think before you respond.* Glib responses and witty remarks are not useful in any kind of salary negotiations. They give the other side the idea that money discussions are not deadly serious as far as you are concerned. That is not true. Creating a casual or nonchalant impression gives the other side an advantage. Do not do that. Honest, direct answers in all business works best. This is especially true for women of all ages and the very young. All a boss needs to name a lower figure and defend it to the death is a hint that these negotiations are not extremely important to you.

• *Keep talking.* If you get in a bind, try to talk yourself out of it. Do not give up and assume that nothing can be changed. Anything and everything can be changed. This is the major problem the inexperienced negotiator has. He or she assumes that discussion is closed because the other party says it is closed. Keep in mind that as long as you are both there, there is a chance to reopen the discussion. Do not panic and do not get up and leave.

• *Build for the future.* If you really want the job, you must convince the other side that you are going to stand up for yourself. You then strengthen your position for your next negotiating session even if you do not get everything you want right now.

Negotiation is a continuing process. You and the prospective boss are going to be negotiating many times in the future if you take the job. You lay the foundation for the kind of relationship the two of you will have at this important session. Most people do not realize this because they count day one as the first day on the job. The boss has already formed his or her initial impression. That is why you cannot let your guard down in the negotiating session.

• *Preserve face on both sides.* The object of negotiation is mutual satisfaction, not scoring points. Strictly speaking, this is not an adversarial process. Therefore, your goal is to end the negotiations with both of you satisfied and no one embarrassed. If the boss loses face, you may not get the new job or keep the present job if you are already on board. If you are embarrassed, you may feel uncomfortable for some time after this particular nightmare occurred. That could make a difference in your performance, not to mention confidence level.

• *You are not responsible for the organization's past.* What the company used to do, what it did to or for anyone else does not necessarily apply to you unless there is a concrete policy. Do not get into discussions about what your predecessor got or did not get. If you agree to be bound by what your predecessor got, or agree to have what you will get influenced by this person, you are abdicating your power to negotiate. Think how easy this makes things for the employer! He or she can simply operate on precedent, one which is nothing like universal. It is the narrowest kind of precedent because it applies only to two or three people under one boss in one department, in one company. Seek to broaden the examples, not narrow them. That kind of insular thinking may also apply to how things are done. Test the water!

Here are some of the specific situations you are likely to meet either in negotiating for a new job or in getting more money in your present situation.

• *The Lockout.* In the final stage of negotiations, the prospect says, "Look, we really need to fill this spot today. The best I can do for you is $14,000 to start, take it or leave it. Why don't you have a cup of coffee across the street, think about it, and come back in an hour." If it is a powerful, older man saying this and you are young, it is especially intimidating, although it can be intimidating at any age. The lockout ploy is designed to make you think you have been dismissed. If you get up and walk across the street for that cup of coffee, you have agreed to two terms. You will say yes or no to the $14,000 and second, you will do so immediately. Do not leave the room. Say to the person, "I really don't feel that I know enough about the job or the financial arrangements to make a choice. In fact, I still have some questions I need to ask you." Then begin asking your questions.

You now have got the negotiations back on a more equal basis. The prospect definitely would have the upper hand if you left. If you stay, the more you talk to this person, the greater the chance to get him or her to move from his or her stated position. By staying you also have a chance to test whether this was truly a final offer or whether it was an opening ploy. Our experience has been that this is most likely an opening ploy. It is not ever a particularly high stakes game for the prospective boss unless he or she wants you very much. If that were the case, this ploy would not be used. He or she can always appear to have been "persuaded" by you to go higher or make some other concession. It is also a very quick strategy because he or she knows within an hour whether you are going to be working there. And if you are not, then he or she will call the next candidate.

It does have some problems for the employer, however. If you are stampeded into making a decision and you agree to the terms, you may change your mind. The commitment is more fragile because you made it under pressure. Furthermore, if once on the job you find even one person in any kind of job who resisted the initial attack and got more money from that boss—always a possibility—you will drown in your own resentment. This sets you up for both performance problems and more job hunting. You will never trust that person again and you may leave at the first opportunity. Some bosses are insensitive to turnover and may not think that employees who stay less than a year means there is a problem.

• *The equity game.* You are negotiating with your present employer or a prospect and you have made a convincing case for a particular starting salary or raise. The other side is in the position of having to agree and to give you the money you have asked for or raise another argument. Most of your case is based on the market rate which is based on fact, not opinion. Finally, the other person says, "Look, I know what you say is true. You meet the qualifications and you are probably worth the money. However, if I start you at that figure (or give you that kind of raise) I'll have problems with all of the other people in the department. They will feel that if you get that kind of money, they're entitled to the same. Maybe we can compromise on half of the difference."

Think before you respond to this. The boss has conceded that you are worth the figure you asked. You are—or likely to be—more productive. This means that you are halfway home. However, you are left with the equity albatross that you will have to pass back to the employer. The key is to ask if the company pays everybody in the same or similar jobs the same rate. The answer will be, "No, of course not." If you work there say, "I thought we had pay ranges to take care of the differences in performance." The boss will agree. The company has made distinctions within jobs. This idea did not originate with you. This does not address the boss's problem because what other employees will think *is* the boss's problem, not yours. After the boss concedes that the organization does value jobs differently, ask if a new employee were brought in from the outside who was making about what you have asked for, would the company ask him or her to take a cut? You are on fairly safe ground here if you are not in a glamour business with minimum-wage pay standards. Most personnel departments constantly advise managers not to hire people for less than they currently make because the people must lower their standard of living to take the job. Most people cannot do this for very long. If the job is not thrilling (no job is thrilling 100 percent of the time) they will move again for more money within less than a year.

The third idea to throw out is that it may actually make people work harder if they know that better performance results in more money. You can express this as either your personal philosophy or something you have observed in the past. You again stand on firm ground because this is the myth structure that underlies the work ethic. Nobody has proven conclusively that better performance always equals more money. In many organizations, performance seems unrelated to the ways money is allocated. Whatever the facts may be, most bosses would not willingly acknowledge that there is no relationship. It would mean debasing a most sacred cow. You will probably be sworn to secrecy about what you are earning, but you may get the money. At the least you will have a chance to decide whether the offer is within your range. If it is not and you are already working there, it may be time to move. If you are not employed you will need to keep looking.

Notice that your behavior never grandstands. You never imply, much less say, that if you do not get what you want, you will not stay, or, if currently employed there, you will leave. These tactics are never useful. They leave a bad taste in the mouth of the other party and never enhance a working relationship. They also raise the boss's need to remind you who is boss and who does have the power.

Above all, whatever you decide, you have got to preserve the working relationship until you can get out or, if you agree to take the job anyway, until you can renegotiate.

• *Entitlement.* Entitlement is a philosophy that grew up in fat days. It says that every employee who has been on the job a certain length of time is entitled for this reason alone to more money. Entitlement may be related to changes in market salary rates or inflation, but it does not have to be. Sound like a good deal? Entitlement works against the productive, that is the catch. While some companies have moved away from entitlement, others hold on, feeling that it simplifies all salary negotiations. This is a variation of the equity game. You and the prospect are talking about salary or you have asked for a raise. The other side says, "Look. We find that what works best for us is paying everybody doing the same job about the same. (Everybody is used loosely here. Do not include upper middle and top management or the sales force.) That way no one is jealous because someone else makes more money. Things are harmonious. If I give you substantially more than someone else, it will get people to thinking about how much they are earning rather than what they are doing."

This is an argument most successful with the young and presumably idealistic. (Fortunately while youth remains, this kind of idealism is on the ropes.) Only someone with little work experience is likely to think that most people do not spend considerable time thinking about what they earn versus what others earn. Your defense is to immediately raise the argument of merit. Ask, "Are you saying that the company does not believe in (or have) a merit system? If not, how does somebody make more money or is that not possible?" The more innocent you appear, the less likely you are to arouse hostility, especially if there is a significant age difference between you and the boss or prospect.

You are putting the other person on the spot but there should be some explanation. If there is no explanation, you will need to rethink your plans about working for this organization. There can be no advancement unless some people make more and others less. There is also no incentive to raise productivity.

The 7 Percent Solution

Even in piecework systems in which what one earns depends solely on one's own efforts, some make more and some less. A variation of this which is actually a ripoff or outright lie is the "X percent across the boards" argument. It goes like this: "We've decided to give everybody seven percent across the boards this year because that's the pot we've got." This is probably not true. What the manager has is 7 percent of the total salaries in his or her fiefdom. If all salaries add up to $100,000 for 10 employees, he or she has $7,000 in the pot. This can be divided any way the manager chooses. It did not come down from top management that each employee, regardless of performance was to get 7 percent. In fact, the opposite was probably true. Top management might prefer that star performers get 10 percent and less stellar ones 4 or even nothing.

Your boss does not want the aggravation, arguments, discomfort, and heavy responsibility of making those choices. He or she is perfectly content with giving everyone the same thing. The people who have done the least they could and still remain on the payroll are unlikely to protest. Only those who have been carrying the less productive are likely to raise a question. If you are one of the carriers you must not disagree with this so much as raise the issue of merit. That is the only argument you have got because it is such a sacred cow. Say, "Are you saying that there is no merit system, just entitlement?" or "Does that mean that no matter how hard you work you'll still get only whatever the group gets?" or "You mean that even if a person is more productive they get the same as someone who's less productive?"

A smart boss is likely to attempt escape by throwing back, "But how do you measure productivity?" You should be prepared to answer, "I understood that was what happened during performance appraisal." Keep in mind that if you had a really foolproof system for measuring productivity, especially in service businesses and service areas, you would not be dickering over nickels and dimes with this boss. You would be a very wealthy consultant with a Park Avenue address. Do not buy any problems that are not your own. Your tone of voice in initially responding and raising questions is vital. Be as dispassionate, as uncritical, as impersonal as possible. You are really just interested in the facts, not in criticizing what the organization or this boss is doing. If the boss becomes defensive, don't do the same. Just say, "I'm sorry, I was just trying to find out what the system was" or "how the system works." If the company does have a pure entitlement system such that merit raises are rarely given or at least in your area, you should be prepared to move. Entitlement raises will always be less, frequently much less, than those possible in merit systems or quasi-merit systems.

• *Future Shocks.* This ploy is aimed at getting you to name a lesser figure than you opening number by pointing out why getting more money now will diminish your prospects in the future. The boss or the prospective boss says, "But if we give you such a large raise or start you so high in the range now, we'll hardly be able to give you anything at the first performance review. You might not get any more money for eighteen months to two years." Be prepared to take the chance. Say, "I realize that might be the case but I'm expecting that my performance will be so good you'll feel differently (or the company will feel differently) in a year." Get the money up front. This is critical. Most raises are a percentage addition to your present salary. The larger the base, the larger the raise you will receive. With inflation, the current dollars you receive are worth about 12 percent more than they will be in a year and about 18 percent more than they will be in 18 months. Studies have shown that the higher in the salary range you start, the higher your salary will continue to be. Certainly most executive recruiters would support this. Therefore, you want to start as high in the range as you can. This may also affect how quickly you move from one grade level to another. If you are bumping your head on the top of the range, you and others may get concerned to move you up a grade. Create some thrust for your own upward mobility. If you start at the very bottom of the range, you have plenty of room to move within that grade and that is not good. It is better to seem to be moving up faster and therefore be more promotable.

• *Passing the Buck.* This is a favorite management ploy. "I'd like to give you what you asked for but my boss wouldn't or doesn't approve." Don't challenge this. Even if the person you're negotiating with has the power to give you what you ask or an increase, if you expose him or her as a liar it will not help your career. You need to question what the two of you together can do to get you more money. Say, "What are *X*'s objections to my getting a raise or this starting salary?" If you are not on board yet, and the prospect does not know, suggest that perhaps you ought to talk further when he or she has found out. If you accept this argument going in, you are agreeing to a buffer between you and whoever does decide on salaries and raises. That means you are negotiating with the wrong person and that you will continue to negotiate with someone who cannot or will not negotiate. Can or do you love the job enough to put up with this? Somewhere else there is a similar job with a boss you can negotiate with. The only reason you would accept this situation would be if something in your personal life kept you from changing today. For example, you or your spouse is seven months pregnant and the company's health plan pays 100 percent of the cost. You will stay until you have had the baby, of course. In two months you are due for a large bonus or profit sharing check. Otherwise, you must either shake the person from this position or find another job.

You can try any of the following:

"Would it help if I put this information in writing so that you could present it to the boss?"

"Do you think there is anything we can do to change his or her mind? For instance, would it help to know that what the organization is paying is not the going rate? Lots of managers would be concerned about this because it means that the organization cannot recruit top talent."

It is possible that either the boss does not think you are that much better or there are so many clones available that getting absolutely the best performer is not important. If either is true you have two choices. You can find a different job or you can begin to sell yourself within the organization to your boss, to his or her boss, and through the grapevine. The problem is that either strategy takes time. However, if you are competent, getting a new job is probably less trouble.

• *Rememberance of Things Past.* This is probably the most popular ploy employers use. It is wonderful because it is so logical and it forces you, as a prospective employee, to think creatively under pressure, never an easy thing to do. The employer asks what you earned on your previous or present job. You say, "I was making $20,000 including a $2,000 annual bonus." The employer says, "Then we'll pay you $23,000. How does that sound?" You are getting a raise and in the prospect's eyes you should be grateful. The trouble is that you were working for a small company at about 20 percent below market. You are going to continue to be underpaid unless you act boldly now. You say, "According to my research, market for this job is $24,000 to $27,000. That's what I'm interested in. One of the reasons I'm leaving the Happy Home Company is that they did not pay market." Since most people think of small companies as paying less money than larger ones, this is a powerful argument. It casts you as businesslike and prudent. Who would stay with an organization that did not pay market? Who would go to work for another one? You do not say this, but the implication is there.

• *Poverty Row.* One of the most manipulative techniques a prospect can use is that which asks you to choose your own interest against those of poor and/or defenseless people. For instance, you are applying for a job with an agency that provides legal services to the poor. The prospective boss says, "We provide services to about 400 families each month. We only wish we could do better than that. As a result, we can only offer you $21,000, even though we know that market is $24,000 to $27,-

000. After all, if you're here you must be interested in helping the less fortunate." But is it tax deductible? That is the thing to keep in mind.

You are being asked to make an involuntary, nondeductible contribution to this agency. You may be expected to work long hours with no overtime and little opportunity for advancement. Before you respond to this, ask about annual reviews and average raises. What you want to know is whether all salaries are the same. Are they on an entitlement system or is there any pretense or merit? If everyone is paid the same and all annual increases are the same, there is a serious problem. You should not take the job even if you talk this person into $24,000.

If there are no differences in salaries you may end up carrying someone who is incompetent. You may be expected to work much harder than others. Knowing the system excludes merit you might decide to coast. That is dangerous to your career. One of the agency's strategies may be to fire the incompetent, bringing someone in at the same figure you were offered, and thus never face the problem of the annual review or longevity. You need to know a lot more about what the salary philosophy is before you get into this job. Part of the agency director's game plan may be a pretense of either "family" or complete candor. Do not treat this as an affront. Test how committed the director is to this philosophy. Don't give up until you get the information you need to make a rational decision.

Ask, "Does everybody start at the same dollar figure?" If the answer is no, ask how differences in starting salaries are determined. Note that you should not affirm nor deny your willingness or desire to aid the poor. You cannot win in that framework and you will end up embarrassing yourself. Obviously the person across the table from you is incapable of embarrassment so that need not be a concern. You must redirect the conversation to the issue at hand which is starting salary.

You may want to ask if it has been the agency's experience

that most people are willing to take less than market. If not, if they have had difficulty in filling these jobs, they may have had to move salaries up toward market. Do not suggest this directly. The implication will carry the idea. You need to find out.

Ask about benefits and pension plans. If there are none or a minimum of these, suggest that you would need more money to provide these services for yourself. Again, do not touch the issue of robbing the poor for your own benefit. You cannot frame an answer to this that will satisfy either of you. Your job is to uncouple your fate from the fate of the poor.

If the prospect brings this issue up again, explain that you could not do the kind of job the agency would want for less than whatever is your bottom line. Yes, you are making a definitive statement. Unless you do this, you have not clarified for the other side what your priorities are. You are not saying that you will not take the job for less than market, only that money affects performance. Are they willing to compromise on performance? The ball is now in the other court.

Even as you talk with the prospect, you are going to have to weigh how much this job is worth to you. You may want it solely for the experience which you expect to turn into significantly more money in 12 to 18 months. If this is true, you should inquire how long someone hired into the same sort of job you are considering stays. If the turnover is very high, then you will know the agency is buying talent as cheaply as possible, providing some training, or more likely the opportunity to learn on the job, and then watching people move on. This is perfectly legitimate from their point of view—how about from yours? This strategy means that you are, or you become, a good job hunter and an active contact seeker. If you are looking for a longer-range project, this may not be the place for you.

Poverty is such an omniscient argument these days that you do not have to be either nonprofit or poor to use it. An individual manager can try to raise the mean guilts when you ask for a raise. Let's say that your current boss says, "I know you deserve a raise. You are doing more than the other people in this department, but if I give you what you deserve, others will go without." Before you respond, ask yourself, "Is this my problem? Am I depressing somebody else's performance?" If the answer to both is a resounding, "No!" then you need to come at the problem differently. Say, "But I thought merit was what the whole salary business was about! Are you saying that no matter how much I do I won't get more money?" If you say this very dispassionately and look your boss in the eye, you will learn one of two things. Either the boss hoped you would buy the gratitude offered and forgo the money, or this was a ploy. Whatever you say, questions are softer than declarations. Ask, do not respond. You need to keep in mind that working relationships are terribly fragile and you do not want to injure this one until you are sure that you are not going to get more money and will need to get a new job.

People using the poverty-row technique also like to use the mean guilts even when reason and merit are on your side. They gamble that you will put aside your own self-interest if they paint a wretched enough picture. The problem is that you cannot be sure that your sacrifice will benefit any of those it is intended to benefit. Furthermore, just as Lee A. Iacocca agreed to work for $1.00 a year as CEO of Chrysler before he asked UAW workers to give up any of their wages or benefits, you have a legitimate interest in who else is sacrificing.

If you do not buy the poverty argument, you will learn something important. You will discover, if you get more money, that this was a ploy. If you do not, you would be smart to conclude that your boss does not value you or your work. Much as you would like to deflect this message, it is very important. How many times will you go through a review only to come out empty-handed? The real question is how much will you have to get from the next employer to make up for the head-in-the-sand approach which you used for several years?

• *The Indefinite Stall.* The trouble with this prospect or boss is that you never get a no. What he or she says is, "You'll have to be patient until I work things out. I can't do it right away. It has to be finessed (with whom?). If you stick with me I'll take care of you." Unless you are on welfare or a candidate for sheltered care, you have got to get this person off dead center. Unless you put some pressure on and suggest a deadline, you may wait years. Your amiable behavior encourages his or her procrastination, not your own financial advancement.

Prospective employers try to get you to take the job at a lower salary on the theory that they will "work" on getting you an early performance and salary review. This, particularly if the organization has a fairly rigid salary system, is a game. If the employer uses this indefinite future reward argument say, "I think it's better to get these things spelled out before we start working together, don't you? That way neither of us will be disappointed." This is not strictly true. If the prospective boss does not snare you with this argument, you can bet he or she will be disappointed!

If your boss promises you a raise one day soon, you can use alternative of choice questioning to try to pin him or her down. "Were you thinking I would get that raise within two months or would it probably be four?" If the answer is, "I can't predict," ask how you can get a better idea of a time frame "so I can budget more effectively." If the boss insists there is no way of knowing, you have learned an important thing. This person lacks either the power or the motivation to give you more money. You are not valued, despite your best efforts. You have two choices. You can begin looking for a way to move within the organization or outside, or you can try to make yourself more valuable to the boss. What you do will usually depend on what you assess as the quicker, more effective strategy.

This same argument can be used to give money without a promotion or title change. This is used frequently with women who, if they acquired more power, might threaten a boss on the status quo. Our research indicates that men are offered this stall less frequently because they are seen as more mobile. Married women hear it the most because after all, "How's she going to get Harry to move—this is the only game in town! She's stuck."

Unless you demonstrate your determination to get the promotion regardless, you will be a victim. After all, if you can be bought off with a 12 percent increase, why should the boss be faulted for doing so?

• *Thunder and Lightning.* Tyranny by temper tantrum is not unknown in many organizations. Reasoning with someone as likely to blow up as Mt. St. Helens is no joy. Of course, you must have *some* reason for being there at all. The problem is how to get more money out of such a creature. Start by praising the person for his reasonableness. Say, "I have something I want to talk to you about, but before we get into that I just wanted you to know how much I enjoy our working relationship. You are so reasonable about things and I know you try to be fair. The problem is . . . ." Say what kind of raise you have got in mind and why. Speak as impersonally as possible and wait for the response. If the boss gets upset and angry, just wait it out. Do not argue or respond in kind. Do not blanche. It is not going to do you any good and it takes your mind off the main event. In effect this is a smoke screen. The boss knows that people become defensive in the face of anger, especially powerful anger. If you become either frightened or defensive you lose. This is a boss who is into Soviet Style or win/lose negotiations. If this has worked in the past, he or she is unlikely to change strategies unless it no longer works.

Many bosses continue to use the same games year after year because the people who stay with the organization and continue to report to the particular boss buy them. You are likely to surprise someone who has had no trouble getting people to agree in the past. Do not expect the prospect to be particularly gracious if you do not prove as malleable as past candidates.

You and he or she may still be able to work together. It will be a judgment call on your part.

Check Gut Responses

Trust your instincts in sizing up the person on the opposite side of the bargaining table or desk. If you do not have a sense that he or she can and will carry out any agreements made, do not decide to plunge and hope for the best. In individual counseling sessions, seminars, workshops, everywhere we get feedback from people, there are those who tell about the frustration, bitterness, and unhappiness they have experienced waiting for someone to make good on a promise or promises. This is not limited to any particular age group, kind of job, size or kind of industry. One common thread appeared. The personnel department was never strong enough to make a manager honor his or her commitments to a subordinate unless not honoring the commitments would have caused legal problems for the organization. The manager usually has total discretion in whether he or she performs. Knowing this, it is difficult to imagine being too careful in screening prospective employers and in reaching very specific agreements with them.

Older managers who have practiced a kind of paternalistic management are likely to balk at anything that they view as reducing management discretion. Stand your ground. The victim is never respected whereas if you are firm you can usually get all or part of what you want. Women are no easier to bargain with than men. Because they frequently have less power than a man in a particular job, they are often reluctant to commit themselves if they are not sure they can carry out a promise. Men are less likely to hint that they cannot deliver or to hesitate for that reason. Many employees report the boss's promising anything necessary to get them on board knowing all the while—obvious in retrospect—that none of the promises could be kept.

There is no protection for the individual negotiator other

than careful preparation up front and taking the process step by step. This historically greatly boosted labor unions. If you need further practice to develop your negotiating skills, check with a community college for courses. If none exist, organize a group of friends with the same problem and do some mock labor negotiations. Individually develop the negotiating grid described in Chapter 5 and then compare answers. Read all that you can. One of the best recent books on negotiating is *You Can Negotiate Anything* by Herb Cohen. It was published in 1980 by Lyle Stuart Inc. of Secaucus, New Jersey. Check the public library and ask the business room librarian for help. Every evening or spare hour you devote to this project will be more than repaid financially and in the confidence you will have in yourself.

Ask friends what kinds of ploys and games they have met while negotiating with employers and prospective employers. Learn from the mistakes they have made. The greatest problem you have as a negotiator will be your limited experience. Learning from others can reduce the surprises you run into. The greater your need to secure your financial future, the more time you will have to spend on this process. There really is no other way.

7

Option One:
The Jump/Shift
External or Internal

You have done everything right. You have worked like a potato bug for two or three years. You have been political and let everyone know you are interested in moving up. Your performance reviews have been excellent. You have gotten two raises in two years, one 7 percent and one 10 percent. As far as you know, those have been top dollar in your department. Your boss says he or she is pushing for you and you have no reason to disbelieve this.

Despite your best efforts you have run into a wall in this organization. You are not going to get a promotion no matter what you and/or your boss do. You are stuck. There may be no possibility of transfer because the company is too small, too spread out, or too technically specialized. This can happen to anyone's career despite the best career planning and management. In an uncertain economy it is even more likely. It is most common in the following situations. If you are facing or suspect you are facing one of these problems, you may want to think about making a change.

• *The company has slowed its growth and management is confused about what to do or reluctant to do anything.* While in or-

dinary times your boss and his or her superior would have sufficient power to promote you, particularly when an opening
occurs, they are shackled because of the company's growth
problem. This problem would not generally be discussed except by top management on the theory that public acknowledgment might upset the troops. You can judge for yourself if
your organization has this problem by looking at the rate of
increase in sales or total revenues. If the rate is less than the
rate of inflation, there is no growth. For instance, if sales increased 3 percent last year, there was no growth. The company
actually shrank at the rate of inflation minus three percent.
The fact that growth is rarely adjusted for inflation makes it
difficult to assess how much growth if any may have occurred.
An even worse sign is the ostrichlike attitude of top management. Having tried all they could think of to change the situation and nudge the curves up, management is now hanging in
the bushes awaiting inspiration. It should go without saying
that if the organization is losing money, the time to move is at
hand. Getting promoted on the Titanic was not a step up.

• *The company is being eyed hungrily by a much larger company
anxious to acquire it.* It would be worse if several big companies
were interested and vying with each other for the honor of
swallowing your employer. Everyone in a position of power is
manning the ramparts trying to stave off this takeover. This is a
gut response that has a lot to do with top management's desire
to remain top management. Your problems and your career
are very low priority right now. If this were a one-, two-, or
three-month proposition, you would await developments. If
the company is badly managed, this could ultimately be a
blessing. The problem is that going through the process is a lot
like major surgery without anesthetic. Unfortunately, this may
go on for more than a year as each group jockeys for position
and tries to improve its leverage. You will need to decide how
long you can wait. Most people are better off making a move
under such conditions. The wait means lost opportunity and if
the wrong side wins the day, you probably will not get the

promotion anyway. Remember how new management likes to "bring in its own team?" If you hang around, you are betting your time and earning power that present management is going to win. This may not be smart. If your boss begins to hint his luncheon dates are all with search firm executives, you may want to abandon your position in favor of a new one elsewhere.

• *Your boss likes you. Inexplicably, your boss's superior is dead set against your being promoted.* There is a limit to the support and help your boss can give your career in the face of his or her boss's opposition. After all, sacrificing his or her career is unlikely to help either of you. You may discover that your boss's support is not as concrete as you had thought, a fact well worth considering. Before you decide to jump ship, you must ask your boss to get as many details on the problem as possible. Do not settle for generalities. "He doesn't think you're ready," is not very specific. Ready for what? "She feels that you aren't the right personality type for that position." What is the right personality type? Much as any of us dislikes the thought, there could be something about you that needs improvement. If you have a personality problem—shyness for instance—you are a candidate for a jump/shift to a higher level job with a boss who finds shy people restful. Do not kid yourself that you will become more outgoing through an act of will. You may become more resentful but probably still quietly resentful.

If your image needs polishing, that can be done with external changes and coaching. Your lifestyle may be too informal or too formal, which can easily be corrected. If, however, what is wanted is a complete personality change, you are much better off moving.

Once you decide that you and the boss's boss have irreconcilable differences, try to assess how long this individual will be around to thwart your career. Maybe you can hang on for a short period. Is the person nearing retirement? Is he or she a likely candidate for a search firm raid? Could you help that process with your contacts? Is he or she in political trouble higher up? Activate the grapevine in other parts of the organization and see what the grapes say. Check with your outside contacts. It may be that the person will not be there forever. It will be a question of how long forever is. How long can you wait?

• *The company likes to bring people in from outside at the level at which you want to be promoted.* They call this bringing in "new blood." Before you try to beat the system, verify that this *is* the system. It may be one boss's aberration. Do not damn the rest of the organization out of hand. There may be internal opportunities. However, if the company is implementing its mixing theory exactly at the spot on the chart in which you are interested, you do have a problem. Unless you are prepared to wait for a change in management philosophy, you will have to move. There is no reason to assume a change is forthcoming unless the organization is in trouble.

The point to giving some thought to all the options before you embark on a move is this. Job hunting is extremely stressful. It is not fun for most people. Therefore, one needs a strong reason to submit the body and mind to that much stress. If you are falling behind financially, you must assess how much longer you can let this continue before you make a change. The best thing is to be promoted internally. Failing that, you are ready for the jump/shift.

Planning the Jump/Shift

The jump/shift is named after a move in bridge that involves shifting bidding suits and raising the bid at the same time. In employment situations it means moving from one organization to another (jump) and up one level at the same time (shift). To do both things at once means maximizing the amount of money you can earn while minimizing time and effort taken to reach that level.

The easiest thing to do is to move up from one step to the next. Unfortunately, in a depressed economy some of the steps you need are not there. This strategy assumes two things. You need to do two things at once because you have fallen significantly behind financially, say 30 percent. You are also concerned that in your present organization it will be years before anything happens. You have already waited too long—say three or four years. If you go to another organization and wait three or four years, you may eventually retire somewhere unpromoted. Hence, there is a certain desperation in your strategy. You have been determined not to move again unless you can significantly better yourself. In order to do this, you must ask yourself the following questions.

• *Do you have the skills to jump up one level?* If so, to what kind and size company would a jump/shift be easiest? If, from day one of your present job you have been not only doing your own work but watching your boss, you should have a fairly good idea of what the boss does. If not the boss, you may have been watching a coworker who is one level up.

What essential skills does the boss use that you do not have or which are not well developed? If the boss spends a lot of time on budgets but you have difficulty reconciling your checkbook, you are not going to be convincing with a prospective employer when you look blank at the mere mention of line items and zero base budgets. It is time for a course in accounting for nonfinancial people or some tutoring from others who are knowledgeable on budgets.

Let us suppose that one of the requirements of your boss's job is the ability to write proposals. Not only are your writing skills very poor, you have no idea how a proposal should be organized or what should be included. It is the same principle as the budget. You can enroll in a seminar or short course on proposal writing or you can find a tutor who will help you develop your skills. In either case you will need fairly intensive practice before you can say with confidence that you know how to write proposals.

Managing people, while a skill, is fairly nebulous. It is even difficult for the very experienced manager to show he or she has done it well. You can use experiences you have had in volunteer organizations to demonstrate these skills. The budget problem requires a familiarity with terminology. That is why it is harder to convince people you can do what you have not done. You need not guess about the skills required.

It may be possible to get your boss's job description or that of someone else whose job sounds interesting. You have to do your own matching between what you have done and what is required. Job descriptions are not standard from company to company, of course, but if you are applying for a job one step up, you need at minimum to be able to speak to the common characteristics these jobs share.

The biggest mistake most people make in assessing how long it will take to learn something is to confuse years of doing the activity with knowing how to do it. Remember that only in the government is the assumption made that if you do something for enough years, you will eventually get it right. In private industry anything that is not licensed or regulated and that can be demonstrated can be accepted as valid experience. If you show some budgets you have prepared as a volunteer and can talk knowledgeably about them, you will not have a problem.

You will be pleasantly surprised to see how much you have absorbed without direct effort just from working at your job. You may find you have no more than one or two deficiencies. This should cause you to shorten your time frame.

This process of checking and sharpening your skills has many benefits. The confidence in knowing that you are the state of the art will give you an edge in interviewing and in selling yourself. It is a risk to make a jump/shift. You might get in over your head. If you have spent sufficient time looking at what you have to work with, you lessen that risk.

• *How are your professional contacts?* If you have been spending your time on internal politics instead of raising visibility in your trade or professional associations, now is the time to mend your fences. Personnel departments are most unsympathetic to risk taking. The jump/shift is a risk not just for you but for the organization. Personnel is not going to be particularly supportive of your desire to skip up a square on the game board. Therefore, as in few other job hunting situations, it is absolutely essential to move around personnel and make your initial contacts only with those who have the power to hire you. You will almost certainly have to dance with personnel somewhere along the line but at least it will not be initially. They will not be able to keep you from proposing your idea to someone who could make it happen.

When Mary Beth decided that she would always be a flunky in the large public relations firm she looked around for contacts who could help her get out. What she wanted to do was to move from PR assistant to account executive with a medium-size firm. She had spent three years working on one kind of product and was bored with it. Every time she would suggest that she really wanted and needed to learn about some other kind of product or service, she was told that she could not be spared. She was "too valuable to her boss." Didn't she understand about specialists? Realizing that, whether it was true or not, there was no way for her to make more money except by broadening her range. She began to talk to friends in the business. In addition to other public relations people, she found the printers' sales people excellent sources of trade gossip. She began to lunch with people at different levels in other kinds of public relations agencies and also those in the PR function in companies. In three months she turned up ten live job leads of which five were promotions. Our research shows that it takes few contacts to produce one live job lead. Once she had decided which jobs were most interesting and fit her plan, it was not a problem to arrange interviews with the people who made the hiring decisions. Had Mary Beth been hungrier, she would have been able to do the same amount of research in three weeks. She stretched it out.

Contacts are essential. The important idea is that the

jump/shift is very hard to work through a personnel department without the assistance of the person who will make the hiring decision. After all, if personnel encourages this sort of thing, who knows where it might end? What helps your case is that while personnel might hint that you were not the most qualified candidate ever to apply, if a particular manager is set on hiring you, it would not be politic for personnel to press its point.

• *What is your plan?* How are you going to sell the idea that you are qualified, if somewhat short on experience, to a stranger? It is best to begin the selling process by maximizing exposure. Spend some time talking to the prospect about the field in general before you explain your game plan. The single most important element in successful selling of any kind is repeated exposure. The prospect needs to see you and get to know you over time. Otherwise no proposal you make will have a receptive audience.

Maximizing your exposure is not as time consuming as it sounds. What is important is that you and the prospect get well enough acquainted that when his or her secretary announces your telephone call, the prospect does not say, "Who?" This may mean talking at two or three association meetings or trade shows or meeting twice and having someone else casually mention your name to the prospect. It is expected that the person has some turnover and that he or she will have jobs from time to time. Why would you be talking to anyone who did not? If this person has a specific job opening that you want, you will need to speed up the timetable. Do not delay applying or letting the prospect know you are interested because you have only met once.

In addition to having done your financial homework as described in Chapter 3, you should have done your organizational homework. What is the prospective company's philosophy? What are the company's long-term prospects? You also need to research the boss. How much time does the average employee stay with this boss? You can find contacts who know, or know of, people who can help. Do not worry about discretion as much as fact gathering. It is no disgrace to investigate before one commits one's time, effort, not to mention stomach lining, to a particular organization and boss. Caution and prudence in an employee are not undesirable qualities. Keep careful notes if you will be talking to a great many people. Otherwise you are likely to confuse yourself.

• *What is your time frame?* Do not wait to begin this process until you are so fed up you are a bomb waiting to explode. One of the most common symptoms stalled people talk about is when they begin to steal pens. You cannot interview under those circumstances. You can get so upset by what you see as your unfair treatment and stalled career, you turn your contacts off. They will not help you if you cannot sell them on helping you. Therefore, if you are beginning to feel that you are stalled and that nothing can or is going to move your boss off dead center, begin looking. There is no percentage in waiting until you are so desperate your judgment is impaired. As one man said, "I knew I had to do something when I began to carry off boxes of BIC pens and one dozen packages of yellow pads. I didn't want them, I was just acting out my resentment and rage."

By the time Roger fully understood how bad business at his engineering consulting firm really was, he was on the verge of panic. He had seen himself as merely stalled, not a candidate for fairly certain unemployment. Instead of concentrating on the jump/shift and using this opportunity to move up and out, he panicked and accepted the first lateral level job he found. His desire to stay on the payroll cost him an opportunity that it took him another two years to get in the new organization. This is very common when people are startled out of complacency by a heavy dose of realism. If you have a plan in the back of your file cabinet for just such emergencies, you would be surprised at the strength it gives you to withstand such emergencies. Roger's company did not fold. One month after he left, they got an enormous new account and declared a bonus at the end of that year. Such are the vagaries of the business world.

• *What are your selling arguments?* The best argument for future performance is always past success in the same activity. As we said, the only big problem with making a jump/shift is convincing someone that ten years' experience in the exact job he or she wants you for is not essential. Therefore, you will write your resume, structure your arguments and concentrate wholly on showing that despite your lack of the specific job title, for example, manager, account executive, salesman, etc., you have done the job. Failing that, you will show you have done parts of the job in a different context. It is important to your strategy to arm yourself for the possible objections people can raise. You need to make sure that everything you say and show (resumes, proposals) reflects your successes in a similar kind of activity.

In addition to a resume, a job proposal can help. Basically, a job proposal explains step-by-step how you fit into a particular job. It is usually one to two pages. It gives you more room to talk about what you have accomplished, and, like the resume, it can be left behind. Naturally a personnel department that has forms for all occasions and a set procedure for each step of the hiring process is not going to be enthused about a job proposal. It is more paper for them to handle. That is the opposite reaction from the one you are likely to get from a prospective boss. He or she is interested in as much information that will help with the choice as possible. Our experience has been that few prospects make up their minds to employ you on the spot. This is normal in any employment situation and since what you want is at variance with custom, there is even more thinking time needed. This is no different from you, the job hunter, who wants some time to think about an offer. You are making a reverse offer. Everything you can leave behind with the prospect increases your chances of making the sale.

A proposal is an ideal opportunity to put into writing all of the connections between what you have done in the past and what you want to do. Concentrate on showing similarities. If the new job calls for budget responsibility that you did not have on the last job, talk about your seminar, your experience as a volunteer, even your interest. The proposal should show connections for between 75 and 80 percent of the job responsibilities. Why that number? If there is not anything new to be learned on the job, you are probably not really moving up. It is a lateral move. You are not going to get a title, which is a gain, if you get the job. However, you are supposed to be thinking in terms of your long-term career. If you are not learning anything except the folkways of this particular organization, then that is not skills development.

Do not apologize for the fact that you cannot do 100 percent at this time. Sell your teachability as an asset. The perfect candidate with the proverbial ten years' experience may cost a great deal more than the company is willing to pay. Someone with 75 percent under his or her belt may offer more enthusiasm, more productivity, and, at the least, will work harder.

Think through as many possible objections as you can that a prospect can raise and prepare written answers. Polish these answers until you feel comfortable with them. This is as much a part of the selling strategy as preparing proposals or convincingly positive arguments.

• *How do you handle salary negotiations?* You should do your salary research not only on starting salaries but on percentage increases the organization gives for promotions. The reason you are going through all of this is the need to do two things at once, thus improving yourself financially with a great leap forward. The absolute dollar amount you ask for will depend on the market and the organization's internal salary structure. There are two strategies. You can research grade levels within the company and make sure you only talk about jobs within that grade level, one or even two higher than your old job. You can ask for a percentage increase which reflects both a percentage for the move and a percentage for the promotion. The easiest transition is to move up one level in an established grade system. These things are defined, and it is easier to negotiate. In small organizations, however, that is not always possible because they have no established grades. Hence the need to be prepared on two fronts.

How can you introduce your salary demands into the conversation gracefully when you are initially screening someone? This is important as you do not want to waste time on a job which, however wonderful, does nothing to improve your situation financially. Therefore, as you and the prospect are getting acquainted and you have a chance to tell what you are looking for, mention the range. Say, "I'm looking for an account executive opportunity in the $20,000 range. Note that you do not close the range. It is too soon to lock yourself in, especially if you have not completed your market financial data.

The Best You Can Do

What if, despite yeoman effort, careful planning, and an exhaustive search, the best you can do within the time you have allowed is either a lateral move with 15 to 20 percent more money, or a significant promotion with very little or no more money? This problem is most likely to occur when there is a surplus of people like you or the economy in the geographic area is depressed. If you are determined to make a move now, or you must move, which is the best choice?

The answer to this will depend on your goals and on your immediate needs. You will want to make a grid comparing what you have now in terms of money, opportunity, security, if that is an issue, and comfort level.

Money

When you evaluate money in this situation, do not neglect the fringe benefits and any hidden costs (see Chapter 3). You must always be careful of gross numbers because you can make a mistake so easily. Include the date of the first salary review in your analysis. In the end the question is whether you think you will eventually make up the 15 or 20 percent or more from the job which changes your job title. There are several ways you might do this. One strategy would be to take the title, do the job for three or four months while continuing to job hunt and selling the new title. Of course, you will not have the use of the 15 or 20 percent of your salary which you would if you took the lateral offer. Can you do without easily or is more money your principal objective?

Opportunity

If you have not had an opportunity to advance in more than five years, the promotion may be necessary. Search firms, especially, are eager for people who have moved upward regularly. If you have been in a job 15 years with nothing but annual salary increases, you will have a difficult time explaining this. The promotion will mean more if it is the first in a long time. However, you will need to consider if the lateral move might entail a promotion in the near future. The issue: Can you afford to take the chance?

There are any number of reasons for having stayed in the same job for a significant period, say more than five to seven years. The job may have changed even if the title has not done so. This can be explained easily on a resume or job proposal. The company may have had an extended period of fighting for its life and you may have been a soldier in that battle. You may have been devoting yourself to other parts of your life and giving only maintenance level attention to your career.

Most important in discussions with prospects is to show that you have a logical explanation for what you have done in the past. It is important to appear to have had a game plan.

Security

Some people really do not like the idea of moving frequently no matter how much progress they make. If you are one of those people, the question is which situation you could live with the longest. Do not kid yourself. If the money would be more important a year from now, go in that direction. If the promotion would be, that is your choice. Think long-range. If you tell yourself that you will move again in three months—and that is actually against all of your inclinations—you are into heavy self-deception.

People who have never thought of themselves as security minded are most likely to make this mistake. If you have only made one or two moves and neither was particularly painful, you may not be prepared for the stress and pure pain of trying to sell yourself aggressively. Always think in terms of the worst thing that could happen. That way you do not have any ugly surprises when you get heavily into job hunting.

Comfort Level

If it will bother you that people will not know you got a big raise but will know you did not get promoted, your choice is clear. You will not feel good about any job which makes you feel you have been diminished in the eyes of your friends. If you look as if you are making no progress, you will eventually come to believe this. Know thyself and do not try to change your gut feeling for a few extra dollars. You cannot.

The only person for whom a wrong choice will have long-term implications is the one who really loathes change to the extent that it will take him or her at least 12 to 18 months to recover from the move. If at all possible wait until you find something you can live with longer term. That does not mean you will stay longer than 12 to 18 months, but you could if you wanted to. The only way either of these situations can be used to help your career is if you expect that you will have to move on fairly quickly, either internally or outside. Particularly in the case of the promotion without an increase, your ability to remain satisfied with the job—if you ever were to begin with— is very small. You are not improving yourself unless you treat this as an interim step.

The jump/shift can take three months to two years to put into effect depending on how quickly you work. If you have many contacts who can help you with live job leads, it is a simple procedure. If you are new in a particular place or have never been active in any business groups, it will take longer.

If you get stuck and seem to find no one willing to consider you for a higher level job based on your present experience, the problem is one of selling. Reexamine the way you are presenting yourself. Do not assume that you need to get an MBA to validate what you know. For some managers, advising people to get MBA's is routine. This seems to be a universal panacea guaranteed (by the universities that offer such degrees) to make all the difference in your career. That is not true. An MBA from a less than stellar institution may even hurt your career. A better strategy would be to change the size and/or type of organization you are targeting. Do not change a basic strategy until you know that it is the strategy that is not working, not some outside interference—the economy for instance. It would probably be difficult to get hired at Chrysler right now no matter how clever you were. Detroit as a job hunting area is much more depressed than Houston. You cannot fault a strategy because most of the organizations in the area are having contractions.

Once more, do not panic. Even if you are temporarily unemployed, it is not the end of the world. It is much worse to be fired for incompetence, insubordination, or sheer goldbricking than to quit because you cannot stand your situation another minute. You can always do night factory work, temporary work, or freelance while you make the right move. Financially you may not be a bit worse off because you will scale down your lifestyle significantly if there is no money coming in.

Retain your flexibility and consider as many options as possible. How do you know what you like if you do not know what there is to like? Explore as many possibilities as possible. Before you make a jump/shift, you should have talked to no fewer than 10 to 20 people. This is an important choice, and you do not want to set yourself up for failure. When in doubt, do not move. Keep looking for an opportunity which, however imperfect, seems to meet most of your needs and does so with some comfort. The object is not only to make a change for more money and a promotion, but to make sure you can succeed in the new environment.

The Internal Move

When Rich looked around his company he was not unhappy with the view. The company was making money, and its long-term prospects were excellent. He was two years away from vesting in the retirement program. He very much agreed with the philosophy of the organization and found the people easy to work with. Most important to him, the office was five minutes from home. It seemed the ideal setup except for one thing. Rich was stagnating as surely as the company was prospering. Even another two years was too long to contemplate staying in that job. There was little turnover in his department and he was at the top of his salary grade. If he moved it would have to be to another department or to a job outside the organization.

When Rich thought over his options it occurred to him that he had very little information about what went on in the organization outside his department other than in those departments he worked with regularly. (This is true of most people in a large organization.) He had spent eight years unwittingly isolated from the workings of the organization as a whole. In order to move internally he'd have to do a lot of homework and quickly. Rich's game plan, as he eventually worked it out, will work for anyone in an organization that is structured hierarchically. Here is the plan.

1. *Start with the company's official organization chart.* These do not strictly reflect reality but they do give you an idea of what the organization *thinks* reality is. Find out about every division, department, unit, and outpost of the organization. Some of these you will discard immediately because they are wholly technical. Accounting and engineering come to mind as unlikely if your area is neither. Once you've decided which areas have possibilities or which you should concentrate on because they sound interesting, these are the things you want to know. The easiest way to organize this information is to have a sheet of paper for every unit of the company you're researching.

Who is the manager or director in charge? You need a specific name. One of the most difficult parts of research is the tedium of having to make many telephone calls to verify what's in the internal telephone directory. Remember that most companies revise their directories about half as often as they should. Verify the names.

What is the particular unit responsible for? Is it a staff or line area? Remember that the easiest move would be to an area that does about what your present department does. Next would be to one that uses some of the same skills as those used in your area. This will probably be the most time consuming part of your research. People who don't know what is going on in their own area are inclined to play expert to someone like you who really needs concrete information. As Rich said, "Deliver me from the people who want to help. My worst problem was the enormous number of bum leads I got. People would say things off the tops of their heads without any real information or personal knowledge. It slowed me down." Remember that someone who has not worked in a particular unit or division is unlikely to know much more than you know or than can be learned from observation.

What is turnover like in the area? This is very important. One of the reasons people stagnate in jobs is that there is little movement, and everybody is there until retirement. It won't help you to set your sights on a new department only to find that it's the ultimate resting place of contented employees. The only possibility would be expansion and that will depend on company policy. Rather than expand the department the company may spin off a new unit.

Is the area a growth area? If the area has not added any new employees in recent memory and has very low turnover you'd better think of other areas with more movement. How are you going to slip into a new department that doesn't need anybody?

What can you find out about the manager? If this person is like your present boss in values and style so much the better. That would make the transition easier. If he or she is very different you will need to proceed with caution. Success and failure are both situational. Our goal in an internal transfer is not to rearrange your personality to fit a new boss but to find a boss who will value you as you are. You might not vest in the retirement program if you got into a new situation in which you failed. That's an important risk and should be uppermost in your mind as you look at opportunities.

2. *Get job descriptions for as many positions as you can.* Even if you don't think you want the job it's important to look at the job description. One of the most successful internal moves you can make is one in which you identify the need, sell it to the appropriate manager, and then fill the job. This is a way of creating your own job and it works very well in growing organizations. These organizations are always a few stages behind in creating and filling jobs to get new tasks done. If you are watching you may be one of the first to notice that something can be done more cheaply or more efficiently than it is being done presently.

3. *Think transferability.* What do you really do on your own job? Not just what your job description says, but what you

have taught yourself to do or added to your job that's not official. Everyone who's been in a job for more than one year has added (and subtracted) things. See Chapter 8 for a complete description of the analysis you'll need to do to catalogue your newly acquired skills. It would be very unusual if about 50 percent of what you do couldn't be used in another job.

4. *Watch the job posting which personnel does.* You may not find your dream job but you'll get a good idea of salary ranges, the kinds of jobs that become available, the frequency of change, and which departments or divisions have the most changes. This is a good check on the accuracy of your research. If you begin to see patterns of activity this can help you in knowing where to concentrate.

5. *Decide what your approach to the personnel department will be.* Personnel can be a tremendous help or a real negative in the internal transfer process. If they act as barriers between you and the managers you need to see, they slow the process down. If they will (and can) give you information about what other divisions do, they are useful.

If you are in marketing services in a consumer goods division and you'd like to try marketing in an industrial division, personnel could be helpful if they gave you names of the people in charge, job descriptions, and pay ranges. This would be a miracle. You'd be more likely to find them hesitant to give you any information that wasn't already in the company handbook. They might give you the page numbers in that book however. If personnel has "rules" that dictate that you are not to approach another division or manager unless you've checked with them first, you are going to have to be very careful. Some personnel departments feel that the only control they can have, outside legal and reporting areas, is to insist that they be consulted by employees, not managers who they can't really control, on internal transfers. We'll show some techniques for circumventing these measures.

Some personnel departments, if they know you want to stay with the company and you have a good work record, will actively try to sell you to other divisions or departments. They will coach you for interviews, talk you up where you're not known, and generally work on your behalf. The acid test is this. Can you find anyone personnel helped or hurt? Ask around among your peers without telling anyone why you want to know. Don't walk into the personnel department and announce your intentions until and unless you are assured by several people with firsthand experience that personnel is at least somewhat likely to be on your side.

6. *Decide on a strategy for dealing with your boss.* If your boss is going to be reluctant to let you go, you will have political problems with long-term reverberations unless you handle this appropriately. It's the same thing as if your spouse or lover came home and announced that he or she were "looking for some new opportunities." There's no way to make that disloyalty palatable unless the boss has agreed up front that you need a move. If you have been very good at your job and made the boss's life very comfortable, it's unlikely that the boss is going to be enthused about your moving on. Therefore, to forestall retaliation it's important to do all of your homework and have some possibilities lined up before you let the boss know you are looking. The chill in the atmosphere once your intentions are known could affect your self-confidence and ability to sell yourself.

If the boss is amenable to your transferring, you may enlist his or her help. One thing which may make the boss more amenable is if you agree to stay until you've thoroughly trained a successor. In some organizations this is a requirement before you can transfer anyway. Don't count on the boss for lots of specific information about areas he or she has no firsthand knowledge of.

The best time to get a reading on the boss's attitude toward your transferring is during a performance appraisal or when you and the boss are talking about your future. If the boss is fairly certain that your future is limited in your present job, you may want to enlist his or her help. If the boss thinks you should stick it out until something turns up, you'll have to be very careful. Remember that just as you use the grapevine to turn up opportunities, there is a management grapevine that could harm you. Knowing your boss's attitude will make a big difference in your strategy.

7. *Use the grapevine to generate opportunities and sell yourself.* One of the combined blessings and curses of every organization is a well-developed internal communications network. If you can use that network effectively, you can benefit from it tremendously. You need to be able to take information from the grapevine and also to put information in.

When you're looking for a transfer, it's important to keep in mind that the grapevine will only be an aid for you if you know what kind of information you want. Don't use the grapevine as a public address system to let all and sundry know that you're looking around. If your boss hears of this, as inevitably must happen, you're likely to find a chill in your relationship.

The best use of the grapevine includes:

Checking on a boss's reputation. You hear from some people that a particular person is "good to work for." From others you hear the opposite. The grapevine can help you find sources outside the company either to confirm or deny these charges. The best people to talk with are those who have left the organization. They are most likely to temper their assessments with some perspective gained by exposure to another or several other organizations. Don't ask how the person liked the boss. Ask him or her to describe the boss's style. Someone else's likes and dislikes aren't important to you unless they exactly match your own. What you need to find out is whether you and this boss can work together. To find that out you will have to find out how the person has functioned in different work situations, especially under pressure.

Hearing that someone is planning to move before he or she has told the boss. If you know that someone is restless you may be able to arrange an interview with the boss even though there is no opening, or so the boss thinks. If you express your interest and sell your abilities you should be the first name that comes to mind when an opening occurs. Don't underestimate this strategy. It is almost foolproof because it has one very powerful element going for it. You may get the job because most bosses so hate the hassle of recruiting a replacement. They may still have to go through the job posting process and interview some people, but it will be perfunctory because they have already made a choice. A boss may even think he thought up the idea alone!

Boosting your own reputation by telling others what you're doing. If you raise your own visibility, some manager may try to recruit you! Think how much that would simplify the transfer process. Don't underestimate the ability of other managers to make the connection. If you seem even slightly interested in moving, someone may approach you. One of the best ways to raise your visibility is to involve yourself in some organization activity that allows you to meet with managers in every area. The Crusade of Mercy, Community Chest, or Blood Drive comes to mind. While no one is anxious to see a solicitor, most people are tolerant of the fact that this is a part of every organization. It allows you to present yourself in a favorable manner and chat for a few minutes with many different people. There is not much competition for these assignments as most employees evaporate when asked to help.

Another way of increasing visibility is to be active in the community. The best activities are those with trade and professional organizations. A political or radical cause won't help you internally. You want yourself pictured as a leader rather than someone who may embarrass the company. Do your own publicity with the local media. If you are an expert in a limited field, this could reduce your options. However, if your topic were how to motivate employees, or increase productivity, or sell ideas, or anything which is generic and therefore important in many departments it can bring you favorable attention. If you're not an accomplished speaker don't despair. Good committee workers get publicity as well.

Finding out what people really do in a particular job. Job descriptions are the merest suggestions of outlines. They don't begin to give accurate descriptions of jobs though they are considerably better than nothing. Even job descriptions that include the percentage of time to be spent on certain activities must be verified. Does the individual really spend that much time on the activity or more? Only the individual doing a particular job can speak to the job content. Everyone else, including the manager, is guessing. A fact of life is that managers are attuned to what is going wrong, not what is right. The individual worker can do almost anything so long as she or he delivers the work packaged to the needs and wants of the manager. The grapevine lets you find and question the people who really know what the job involves. This also gives you something to say in an interview when a manager says, "What makes you think you can do this job?"

You must work systematically at information gathering. Until people realize that your interest is continuing and that you really want to know what's going on, you're not going to get much specific information. You are likely to get generalities. Therefore you can expect to spend many coffee and lunch breaks talking with people, checking and cross checking facts. The telling incident that shakes your assumptions or causes you to rethink an opportunity rarely appears in the first conversation. If you have spent eight molelike years it will take at least a few months for people to accept your emergence from the woodwork and include you in the network.

On the Titanic

All of these suggestions are predicated on the idea that the company is prosperous. There is less chance of any kind of transfer if the company is on the ropes. However, one significant opportunity for internal moves when a company is sick does exist. If you are able to put two or more jobs together and do them because you have more than one set of skills, this can provide an internal move up.

Suppose the marketing department is about to be combined with a sales support department. If you can show that you can do both, you might be in a better position to move ahead of those whose only interest and experience are with one or the other. If you can see a way to combine two jobs or to add some new area to your present job, you can negotiate this exactly as you would a new job within or outside the company. It is a new job. You'll have to write a job description and be prepared to show the feasibility of such a combination. As opposed to staying where you are, this strategy has many advantages. It is the best shot at enlarging or changing your job internally. It provides some opportunity to learn new skills in case the company decides to eliminate the department or departments entirely.

If you have enlarged your job this can be a selling point if you're forced to make a quick move. Don't underestimate peoples' response to initiative. Many managers want to see that you've done more than keep the chair warm for eight years, particularly if the company is trying to raise productivity per salary dollar.

Expect that the internal transfer will take longer than job hunting outside because you must be so much more careful whom you ask what. There is a need to spend more time verifying information than would be necessary with strangers. Still, the need to cover yourself in the future with a retirement plan means that you should never throw eight years of effort toward vesting away without a compelling reason. A reason that compelling would have to be an impending nervous breakdown from the stress, even then it would be worthwhile to ask about medical disability. The only other reason would be a job offer that fit like a glove and included an equity position, possibly a chance to buy stock or to buy in to the business. Even then, those opportunities always exist. Why not get vested and then find a job with equity possibilities?

One of the major changes in employee attitudes since 1977 has been the realization that most of us will live into our old age. That means that either you have a self-managed retirement plan, IRA, or Keogh; you are putting money into your own investment portfolio; or you are going to stay somewhere long enough to vest in a company plan. All three, at different stages in your career, have advantages. The internal transfer helps the company vesting option. Don't throw it away until you're sure that is the best choice.

8

Option Two:
Skills Transfers or
What's in a Name?

For teachers from preschool through college, social workers, some government workers (likely to be more if President Ronald Reagan has his way), association people and others whose salaries are set, often very unrealistically, by hard pressed boards, commissions, and associations, there is hope. You do not have to endure on the hope that the baby boom crowd will decide to have babies themselves or that units of government will realize that you must eat, too. Arise, victim of the nonprofit environment and look around you. There is a way out of your career cul-de-sac. You have nothing to lose but your poverty. The opportunities to transfer from the nonprofit to the profit abound. You can make the leap from a fixed income job to one which has some chance of providing upward mobility and an upward salary curve.

It is difficult to blame boards of education and municipal government for their financial mistreatment of teachers, social workers, and other employees. After all, someone has got to pay for all of those empty classrooms, taxpayer revolts, and welfare cutbacks, and it looks as if you have been selected. If you are a teacher, you will be particularly pleased to know that the numbers now enrolled in colleges and departments of education countrywide indicate that even with the decline in the birth rate, there will be a teacher shortage in the fall of 1982 or 1983. Unfortunately, there is no indication that teachers will be paid more for their work or that cost of living will have anything to do with what they are paid. The same is true of social workers. There may be more openings for social workers as more leave the field and fewer enter. That does not necessarily mean that salaries will be any higher. Most employers of teachers and social workers assume that there will always be a certain number of people who will be willing to work in these fields for very low wages verging on unwilling volunteerism. If you have decided that you are not one of P. T. Barnum's latter day converts, you can get a much better paying job in industry than the one you now hold in the nonprofit world provided two things are true.

1. You must be willing to invest considerable time up front in both discovering your marketable skills and in developing the contacts needed to make the transfer. You cannot do this in one summer while you develop your athletic skills and spend two months on a busman's holiday in Europe or Mexico. If you are a social worker or government worker with scant time off, you are going to have to spend some time every day (and evening) working on your skills transfer.

2. You have not been "just getting by" in your present job. If you have been in the mental off mode, you will have significant problems getting anyone to take a chance on you. Part of this may be attitude. If your attitude toward job or career change is, "Will it hurt?" or "Will I have to give up anything?" the skills transfer is not for you. Instead, direct all your attention to lashing yourself to the organization that now employs you. You have neither the stomach nor the energy to make a career change.

The Career Changer's Quiz

How can you test whether you would be a candidate for a career change? Answer the following questions.

1. *How many times have you talked about career change only to conclude that aside from pay, you are really pleased with what you do?* If you like everything about your job except the pay, you may want to think about how you can restructure your job, to move up even within the limited area available to you. Even in the most depressed market there is some mobility. Your lack of enthusiasm for change will not make you attractive to another organization. If the teacher shortage materializes because others no longer see teaching as an attractive career, there may be openings at *all* levels. Therefore, you will be fighting an uphill battle. Greed alone will not carry you.

2. *Is your principal attraction to the nonprofit organization that it appears to offer security to those who pay their dues?* If this is what you have as a top priority, you are unlikely to find the same degree of job security anywhere outside the Japanese look alike companies—quite rare and likely to remain so in the 1980s. If job security is your top priority, you have made the choice of security over money. However, you would be smart to do some strategic planning and test your assumptions about the future of the school district, branch of government or association you work for to see if these assumptions have any validity. You will really be upset if your organization curls its toes after you have counted on its being there for the duration.

3. *Do you frankly dislike change?* The principal attraction of your present job is that you have it entirely under your belt. There is nothing new to learn or to be done, only refinements of your art. Career change would be very difficult and probably successful only if you were forced by economic necessity to change. Some people see change as instability, not opportu-

nity. If this is your mind set, career change should be a last resort.

4. *Are you stagnating?* You have pushed down this thought a thousand times but it keeps surfacing. You have not learned, thought, or done a new thing in years. You are bored and afraid that others may notice. You may need a career change just to protect your mental health. You might also find yourself a candidate for severe burnout when your boredom reaches a terminal level. Burnout sneaks up on people who find themselves stagnating.

5. *Does your dwindling buying power make you constantly resentful?* Resentment may never have killed anyone, as jealousy and lust are thought to have, but nobody has suggested that it has been healthy, either. The first sign of an employee who is resentful is the well-worn job description. If you say, "I'd like to help, but this isn't my job," with some frequency, you have a resentment problem. The other most common phrase is, "They are lucky we do anything for what we're being paid." Management will not share this view. Despite the concept of complete job security, some managers may resort to other tactics to encourage you to look elsewhere. At any rate, you will pay both emotionally and professionally for such an attitude. If you care about your career at all, you cannot let galloping resentment overtake you.

6. *Are you nearing retirement and already fully vested in the retirement plan?* You may be looking for an opportunity to vest in someone else's plan. After all, if you are at the top of the salary schedule which is the basis for calculating your retirement pay, what you can retire with may be set. You are only 50, so if you got another job and stayed 10 years you would be vested in a new company at 60. Alternately, if you went to work for a smaller company with no formal pension plan you could set up one of your own that might be even better.

7. *Do you need more cash now?* You have twins starting at the most expensive private college in America in the fall. They

are both premed. It is January. If you are going to eat something more than mush for the next four plus years, it would pay to vastly improve cash flow. Hitting it rich in Las Vegas would be nice, but a job that paid more is less risky.

8. *Is it time to change?* You cannot ethically continue to do what you no longer believe either valuable or worth your time. If you do not change you will end up sabotaging yourself.

Sometimes this loss of enthusiasm looks like burnout. If you have rationally decided that what you do is no longer worth doing, it is time to move on before you are asked to do so.

If you answered yes to the first three questions, career change should be on your option list but not at the top of the list. If you answered yes to four through eight, that is a green light to start exploring.

How Much Change?

Once you decide that you owe it to yourself to at least think about changing fields, you need to ask yourself how extensive a change you want to make. There are two principal ways to make a change. You can change areas. You use the same skills you used as a teacher, government worker, whatever, but you use them in the service of some other objective in a different kind of organization. This is not a radical change. The second kind involves changing the skills you use, not just the workplace. Perhaps you are tired of teaching people to do things. What you want is not to use teaching skills but to use your skills in organizing, selling, and in thinking abstractly. Thus, you are making a two-stage, rather than a one-stage career change. You are going to need to spend time assessing how strong your skills are outside the teaching area, and then spend time preparing to sell them.

In Chapter 3 we talked about researching salary levels. This information is very important to you. Before you decide what kind of job you want, it would be useful to decide the kind of industry you would like to get into. Remember that it is possible to use your skills across a broad spectrum, despite industry, location, size, or style. If you want to use them to maximize your salary, it is necessary to pick a growth industry. It is the same thing as investing in the stock market. This does not affect your choice of jobs so much as your choice of arenas. It is a where, not a what question. You will not feel your career change was worth the anguish if you end up no better off financially than you were in your old nonprofit job.

Research Sources

If you have not got a clue as to where you would like to work or what you would like to do, go directly to your business librarian and ask to see a copy of the *Guide to Business and Trade Periodicals* published monthly by Standard Rate and Data Service. This valuable publication lists almost all of the thousands of trade and business publications published in this country. It indexes them by subject matter and by magazine title. Suppose you had always thought you would like to work for an airline but the only jobs you can think of are as a pilot, flight attendant, or baggage handler and no one of these seems to fit your skills. If you call the personnel office of an airline and ask them for the names of other jobs in the organization, you are likely to get a brochure through the mail describing the airline's overall virtues. This will not particularly help you. On the other hand, if you look under airline or air travel in the SRDS guide, you are likely to find a number of publications directed to different audiences of workers within the industry. Each entry in the guide has a publisher's statement at the top which tells what readership the publication serves. This statement can give you a clue as to whether it is worth looking at the magazine itself. If you find one directed to an audience you would like to know more about, ask the librarian for back issues.

The greatest thing about trade and business publications is that they are loaded with information of value to career changers. Most of the articles talk about "what I did and how I did it." They are full of feature stories about people who are stars in their particular businesses (future employers perhaps?). Often there are reports of trade and association meetings to be held. These are always sources of contacts. There is nothing more important to your prospecting than getting a genuine sense of what the issues are in a particular field. For instance, if you were interested in personnel work it would be critical to know what issues are agitating the working professional right now. How is the field changing? Is there anything going on to which you might make a contribution? The trade books give you this kind of information because they are constantly talking about, researching, and surveying to find the issues.

They are full of jargon which, since you are reading instead of listening, you have a chance to see in context and puzzle out the meaning. The difference between an aspiring amateur and one of the "in" group in many industries is jargon. If you know and can use the jargon, it is much easier to convince people that you know enough about the area to make a contribution. For example, the major difference between teaching adolescents and adults in colleges and teaching adults in corporations is language. In schools it's called teaching and in corporations the same thing is called training. Despite the fact that managers of training departments insist that really what they do is more than "just" teaching, there are enough former teachers doing training to prove that the transition is not impossible.

A teacher set on making the move to industry will have to develop contacts within training departments and sell her- or himself to the people who can hire. It rarely is useful to talk to the personnel department per se because they naturally want to hire people whose experience has been in the exact specialty.

In the past few years, a number of large corporations have established programs to teach basic language skills to new employees. These programs are not different from the kind of language skills programs offered by inner city high schools except that the companies that offer the same thing apparently feel the first dose didn't take! They are redoing the same kind of programs in an effort to bring new employees up to speed. The transition from teaching basic skills in a high school to teaching the same material in a corporation is the easiest kind of transition to make. It is purely a matter of where one works, not what one does. Many teachers we've talked to report that the students who are being paid to learn do indeed learn more quickly and with considerably more enthusiasm than the same student with the same level of skill in a public high school. This makes the teacher's task considerably easier.

Social workers in drug abuse programs are not much different functionally than employee assistance specialists who help troubled employees through referrals to those very programs the nonprofits run. The parallels are endless. The association person who is involved in member services has a career clone in customer service, subscription services, or any variety of jobs that provide the equivalent service in a company. For most people, the problem is selling the similarities, not lacking the skills.

If you talk to the people you know who are doing a particular kind of job and ask them what they do, as opposed to what they are called, you'll find one interesting thing. Most cannot get beyond what they are called, secretary, teacher, or engineer to describe functionally what they do. They have never thought about it at all. The job title is what is important.

That's a problem. The only way a teacher, secretary, engineer, accountant, or any fairly well-defined job can be analyzed is by looking at its duties rather than at the title. Every job title is really an umbrella capable of covering an enormous number of different, unrelated functions. People shape jobs as they work. Nobody works in a straight jacket. Once you know what you actually do as opposed to what you are called you can begin showing a specific employer why what you have done can be useful to him or her. While personnel departments are frequently obsessed with job titles, most bosses are more relaxed. They have often had a number of jobs that were related functionally but each one had a very different title. Another reason is to learn to job hunt without having to use personnel.

Once you have decided that a particular industry—or to be on the safe side—several industries look interesting, you can rev up your contacts and ask for specific information. Find the trade association that serves that industry and begin making contacts within companies. Your job will be much like the research needed to get specific salary information—tedious and time consuming. The more you know about the industry, individual companies, and finally jobs within those individual companies, the quicker you are likely to be hired. No one has described this process better than Richard Bolles in *What Color Is Your Parachute?* published by Ten Speed Press and available in all bookstores. The book is updated frequently, so buy the latest edition.

If you have been rolling along in a rut for some years, you may have given very little thought to what you *could* do. Your attention has been focused on what you actually do. If so, skills analysis can help you in developing some idea of what you would like to do next if you have decided that you want either a major or minor career change.

Beginning Skills Analysis

Skills analysis involves an inventory and sorting process. If you were planning to rearrange your personal collection of books you would start with at least a partial inventory just to see what you have in stock. Skills analysis begins with an inventory in the same say. You are trying to answer two questions: (1) What skills do I have? This is not the same question as what do I like or what do I do best. It is purely a pulling together of resources. You will decide what you like and do best after the inventory. (2) What are my strengths and weaknesses? There is no point in trying to sell your weaknesses. Concentrate on the things you do well. You need to know your weaknesses because unless you are aware of them, you may sell yourself into the wrong job.

The easiest way to do it is to begin keeping track, in writing, of what you really do on your job. This is the information that will be the basis of your inventory and eventually your resume.

Task	Procedure	Skills Used
1. Taking attendance in classroom	Checking to see if seats are filled with proper bodies	Counting, sorting, recognition of individuals, testing assumptions, making judgments
2. Lesson planning	Deciding on the content, order of presentation, organization of material	Research, writing skills, logic, planning, organization of material, developing examples, presentation techniques, selling the ideas
3. Grading papers	Deciding whether the paper meets the assignment and how well	Developing criteria for judgment, evaluating results, prioritizing results, modifying judgments
4.		
5.		

You can use this format for any job. The important thing is that you do it thoroughly for each one. You will probably have as many as 50 tasks per job and certainly no fewer than thirty. That's why it is so important to do this on a daily basis. If you try to think of all the tasks without some means of breaking them down into manageable units you are bound to skip some. The more dissatisfied you are with what you do, the more anxious you are to make a change, the more important this process becomes.

Write the task you are engaged in, the procedures it takes to do that task, and finally the skills you need to do the procedures. Procedures, as you can see from the examples, mean step-by-step or definition of task. The important idea is to do this over a long enough period of time, usually two days to two weeks, to give you a complete inventory of the tasks you actually perform on your job.

If you have had other jobs or your present job has changed over the years—this is very common—make out such a form for each of these jobs or changes. Yes, you will have masses of raw material. This is a time-consuming, ugly, repetitious, aggravating procedure. It is also absolutely vital. If there were a test you could take we'd certainly tell you about it. Most vocational tests have the value of snake oil and waste time and money. The issue for you is how can you find out what you have to choose from unless you do a complete inventory?

Do not ignore your volunteer work. The measure of work is whether it uses energy, not whether you are paid. The fashion of downgrading volunteer work as "just" volunteer work begs the question. Did you learn anything which can be transferred to a different context?

The mother of a recalcitrant toddler is working, and hard, judged by the amount of energy she expends. She is not paid in cash. You can sell skills developed solely through volunteer work *if* you can show two things: (1) what you did, and (2) the result.

Volunteer Work *Is* Work

Many people undervalue volunteer work because they think that if there is no money exchanged there is no value to the job.

This is not true and it is up to you to show the parallels between what you did for free and what you could do for money. For instance, if you develop a procedure manual as a guide for the officers of a nonprofit group, you'll cover much of the same ground that you'd cover in the same document in a company. Your problem is not the quality of the work or the relevance of it as much as the need to sell what you've done. It is very important to collect samples of the things you've done even if those samples aren't beautiful and slick. Prospective employers are often as impressed by volume as by quality.

There is no volunteer job that can't be included in your inventory if it had a result. A result means that something changed, improved, ceased, or otherwise came about. The bottom line is the change, not the quantity. It's frequently easier to raise large sums of money from the wealthy than to pry money out of the middle class dollar by dollar. The process is the same. Your job is not to blush because you've been active in Boy Scouts but to sell its practical value to an employer. It's not just the name of some of these organizations that sells, it's the work you did for them.

How do you find out what skills you are most proficient in? You cannot rely on your boss's attitude alone because he or she may be responding to your packaging, selling, and political skills as much as to the specific skills. You will need to talk with your peers in other organizations to determine what is an acceptable level of skill in a certain activity as well as what constitutes an outstanding performance. If people have always told you that you are "good with people" you will still want to check this out. What does "good with people" mean? Can this be transferred to another job?

The magical phrase for the 1980s is quality control. You are essentially your own monitor of personal productivity and quality control for what you do. The more interaction you have with job peers in other organizations the easier it will be for you to get a broader look at and understanding of what is quality work in your area. For instance, if you are engaged in selling word processing equipment, what is the measure of success in that field? Is it purely how many pieces of equipment are sold? Does it also involve a measure of repeat business?

If you are a secretary looking for a way out of the area of personal servitude, what is the measure of success as a secretary? What have the people who preceded you in the job gone on to? Is there anything in your job that is readily transferable?

Without absolute guidelines—no field has these—the only way we have of measuring quality of work and productivity is in relation to someone else or to a group of others. This is so important that many companies are now trying to do it formally, through internal peer measurement. You need to make at least a start in comparing your own performance with those of people who do the same or similar jobs in your own company or close competitors. You will find many people willing to participate because it's important to virtually everyone. Ask for assistance and explain the benefits to them of their cooperation.

Don't expect to find definite confirmation of your skill in a particular area. It's enough if you act and react about as well as or slightly better than your job peers. While it's hard for you to measure your own performance it's no easier for anyone else.

Putting the Results Together

Once you have got your raw data, you will need to analyze it four ways.

• *What are the most frequently mentioned skills?* One of the amazing things about people at work is how cleverly they arrange their jobs to do what they like to do. For instance, a social worker whose major work satisfaction is interaction with people always arranges to slight paperwork, even if it sometimes affects a performance appraisal, in favor of more people contact. The association professional who really enjoys contact with the members and the political push and shove on the member side will arrange to insert him- or herself into the fray.

You will be amazed at the ingenuous methods you have developed to do more frequently what you like to do or at least what is less obnoxious.

As you're counting how often you have used certain skills, be sure to look at the context. If organizing comes up 50 times, it is important to say what kind of organizing. Were you organizing people, time, things, ideas, or a combination of these? You may discover that you have spent much time organizing ideas but little organizing time.

For instance, if you have always been very good at organizing people in groups, this needs to be specified. You can't sell any prospective employer on the notion that you're good at organizing in general. You need to be able to give examples of what you've organized and why and what was the result. If you organized all of the social workers in the family services area into study/continuing education groups, you'll need to be able to talk about that as a specific organizing function.

If you have been very good at organizing data and simplifying paperwork you will want to make note of that specifically. An employer who will hire you because of your outstanding skills in organizing data would not necessarily value your skills in organizing people to the same degree.

You also need to be able to see patterns. You may be surprised to find that you have always been very good with data but not so good with, or interested in, people. This is going to be very important information when you begin to explore different jobs and industries, so be scrupulously specific.

• *Putting frequency aside for a moment, what skills have you most enjoyed using?* What you most enjoy may match frequency, but it may not. Part of your discontent with your present job may be that there is no match. Promise yourself that you will consider the skills you most enjoy using as primary as you restructure your career. There truly is no use trying to compete when you are lukewarm. You will not be able to compete with people who love what they do when you are only doing what you think you are good at.

One of the tragedies of the boom in accounting studies is that a great many people who major in accountancy in college, or return for the necessary courses to take the CPA examination, are not interested in what accountants spend their time doing. The same is true of computer science and some branches of engineering. What they want is what they have heard each of these fields supplies: a fast track to the top of the organization. Imagine their surprise when they find that in order to run in the fast lane, you have to love accounting or computers or engineering. A mild interest will not make you competitive with people for whom that field is a passion. Your competitors may not have picked the field because someone told them they'd be good at it or "this is what's really hot right now."

• *What skills do you feel you are most proficient in?* If this list is very different from the other two, you have an interesting problem. You are trying to make a living with your second-best skills. No wonder you are not pleased nor making as much money as you could! It is time to look at the areas of greatest strength and decide where you can best deploy those.

• *The final list should include the skills you are going to use on your next job.* These skills are the ones that any job you seriously consider must use 75 percent of the time. We are not interested in maximizing money alone; job satisfaction is very important. If you are not using the skills you most enjoy and which represent your strengths, you are not competitive and that has a major impact on your earning power.

Avoid the Hot/Hots

The greatest temptation for the career changer is to try to find out what is "hot" in the market. You'd be much more competitive to concentrate on what you do best and most enjoy and then look for a job doing only that. No one but you can make the connection with a particular job. You'll get no help from an employer or from a personnel department. You must not only show the connection but sell it as an advantage to the organization.

When Janet left social work, the last thing she wanted to do ever again was work with the poor or the disturbed, or both. When she did her skills analysis, she found that her strengths and interests were in one-on-one counseling. No matter how she rearranged her data, this was her greatest skill. It occurred to her, after she had talked to a great many people in all kinds of counseling that what she really liked was researching a person's problem and offering some strategies for getting around the problem. In fact, her people skills were not nearly as good as her planning and research skills. However, who is going to believe that a social worker has research and planning skills useful to a business?

She talked to dozens of people and had dozens of information interviews, but not a single job offer. She began to think seriously that her only option was to return to school and get an MBA. At least she would have demonstrated her serious intent. She balked at the two-year commitment and the need to take many courses about which the kindest thing that could be said would be that they kept mentally bewildered faculty members off welfare.

Finally she decided that she would have to demonstrate her skills in a way that a business could understand, obviously that meant in the service of a business. She targeted several small businesses that could use planning and research skills. She designed and conducted some research for each and produced a report. She wrote an article for the city newspaper on trends she identified. She was beginning her own business, even though she had not been able to charge anyone for her services yet.

She then sold a slightly larger company a project just like the ones she had done for free. The entire process took three months. Again she did some publicity for herself and the client. In the end she got a job as a strategic planner with a medium-size bank. While the bank would have preferred a

Harvard MBA, they gladly settled for Janet who could show the results of her work. She got a 32 percent increase from her salary as a social worker. If Janet decides to get an MBA, it will not be because no one will hire her without it. She will have made the decision because she wants the information such a program can offer.

Robert spent 20 years teaching woodworking in a junior high school only to have the program cut. He had reached the top of the public school salary schedule at $27,500, and he faced the prospect of putting three of his children through college within five years. His wife had resumed her career three years before, which had helped the family budget, but it was going to need more help before the middle child graduated from college. Faced with the need to redeploy his skills, Robert made an interesting discovery—12- to 15-year-olds did not interest him nearly as much as tools. In some ways kids got in the way of the fun he had with tools and with the raw materials. Not particularly assertive and certainly nobody's idea of a salesman, Robert decided that there must be a spot for someone in industry with his skills. Since the alternative was fairly stark, it was at least worth looking into. He began to talk to his suppliers and a connection was made. Robert ended up as head of the lumber supplier's sales force. His job paid $32,500 plus a bonus and involved attending trade shows, calling on lumber yards, discount warehouses, and other outlets that sold do-it-yourself products. The company was growing at a rate to make the bonuses lucrative as well as the stock options. Three years after his switch, Robert earned $47,000 including $8,000 in bonuses. He is not unhappy with the change.

There are always barriers to career change. The most important is the lack of a clear need to make a change. Second is the understandable desire not to put so much at risk. Fear is a tremendous obstacle for those who prize job security and think they have it, even as they know intellectually the blow is coming.

If you care about your financial future, it is necessary to see what choices you really have. Maybe you truly are trapped. There is no more money to be made and no other job you could possibly get. Prove it by doing the research. The economy may be bad and your job hunting skills limited, but consider three things.

1. Almost everyone who is knowledgeable at all about career counseling agrees that career change is on the increase and much less unusual than it was five years ago.

2. With much less upward thrust from expansion in all kinds of organizations, it is difficult to get raises that keep pace without a job change or promotion.

3. You have nothing to lose in the effort to get the highest dollar return on your time and talent you can. If you are selling yourself cheap, who is benefiting and why?

Finally, you might try thinking of yourself not as a job title but as a windshield wiper. If you think of yourself as one thing, social worker, teacher, nurse, or association executive, what flights of fancy must you summon to imagine yourself in another role or another theatre? Consider instead the windshield wiper. It is anchored to the vehicle by a solid core, yet it moves over a fairly wide area. You are anchored by a solid core of skills that limit what you can do. Yet, like the windshield wiper, you can range left or right stopping anywhere along that arc that meets your immediate needs.

The windshield wiper idea has a second major advantage. It allows you to be much more responsive to market changes. If social workers in the nonprofit sector are working for less than a living wage, how are they doing in companies? How are the ones who've decided to use their skills as trainers, sales people, administrators, etc. doing? If you have a commitment to one job title only, you are on a ladder that may be going nowhere. If no one wants anyone with that title right now, or wants to pay them very poorly as is more likely, you are stuck.

Your commitment must be to your skills, not to a job title, profession, or industry if you want to do well in the 1980s. If you are not flexible enough to move within your skills arc, you will end up trapped by your inflexibility in a job whose earning potential is vastly outstripped by inflation. Remember this. You can always move back to the nonprofit environment with style if things improve there. The move from one sector to another is not final until you die or retire.

9

Companies in Crisis

Trapped and strapped, there you stand in the worst possible negotiating position. You can't change jobs and your company is going through a crisis that seems never ending. Everywhere you look the news is bad. In the past month ten people you know have left. As one of your closer friends said as he bailed out, "If I were you, I'd cut my losses."

The trouble is you simply can't move right now. For instance, you've been through a tough divorce which has left you desperate for some stability. Another major upheaval would do you in. You are facing a medical crisis and you need your health insurance. You can't risk losing that. You've changed jobs so often you cannot bear the thought of job hunting and fear you'd faint in an interview. Whatever the problem, changing jobs right now would create a stress overload. Don't despair. Depending on the kind of crisis the company is facing, you may not have to change this minute. You may be able to hold on for as much as two years and even improve your situation. Warning: This is no time to hope that retreat and a low profile will save you. A company in crisis is likely to axe the people who don't seem to be the type to make a fuss. Don't forget that you are fighting a survival game. If you don't treat this as a crisis you are likely to be a victim.

The Business Crises

There is a life cycle to business crises that includes a beginning, middle, climax or turning point, and an end. The beginnings usually seem to be a generalized uncertainty. Management stalls, the grapevine heats up, and nobody seems capable of making the simplest decision without great discussion. Beginnings also flush out all of those people to whom any kind of trouble, change, or uncertainty is anathema. There is a general unrest from the mailroom to the boardroom.

The middle is usually a period of calm. The managers and the more aware troops are exhausted and the middle is the period that they use to recharge their batteries. The middle can fool the unsuspecting into thinking that the crisis is over. Be wary of management which says that, "We've weathered the storm," but nothing has changed as far as you can see. This is a sign of the middle period.

The climax usually looks like the resumption of hostilities. It need not be started by anything or any one event. One Monday everybody is back to battle stations as if by common consent. Top management may have decided on a new strategy or, if the company is under siege, the other side may have begun a new tactic. The most important sign of a climax or turning point is that there will be major changes in policies or personnel.

The ending may be the beginning of a new organization, but it usually spells the end of the current power structure or substantial changes in that structure. There can be no resumption of business as usual until the power structure is reshaped. That is a major concern to you because it means that many of the promises which your boss or boss's boss make are not valid. The people making those promises have not got the power to carry through. That's why, needing more money and unable to move, you must be more than ordinarily watchful if you're to survive and move ahead in any of these situations.

We are going to deal with the five most common kinds of business crises as they affect the insider seeking to protect his or her earning power and/or move up. All of these crises carry high risk for anyone trying to come through in better shape than under the precrisis regime. Managers are more reluctant to make decisions. You have to sell harder. You are going to have morale problems as you watch people you like and have worked closely with move out of the organization in panic or worse, involuntarily. If you allow the injustice—real or imagined—of this situation to infect your thinking you have no hope at all. You will be at the mercy of whatever winds blow through the organization. If you truly are in need of your job and unable to move, you are increasing the risk of involuntary severance from the organization.

Five Common Crises

These crises are: (1) the friendly merger; (2) the reorganization during which at least one-quarter of top management is replaced; (3) the unfriendly takeover which management resists; (4) a change in company philosophy, direction, or product line; and (5) gradual or precipitous unprofitability. Each one makes it difficult for the nonmobile to get more money, but it's not impossible if you're willing to plan and to take risks. Nonprofits go through these same upheavals but use different terminology. Beware the person in a nonprofit who seems convinced that everything will turn out. Either this individual has already secured his or her flanks or doesn't understand what's happening.

Keep in mind that the vast majority of people hate change. They may see it as a threat, an inconvenience, as something unfair, a plot, almost anything but an opportunity. Unless you can see the opportunity in what's going on in your company, you may react in fright rather than in a way that helps you maximize promotion and salary opportunities.

The Merger

You have known for some time that the company's owners were looking for some way to expand. They want to find a merger partner, not take over someone or be taken over. It's supposed to be business as usual while the owners check out people they'd like to get together with. In fact, everything is on hold. In an effort to keep the employees from "worrying," management is denying that anything is happening or may happen.

A certain percentage of the people in the organization pull in their horns at the first sign of any change. The result is the organization is not functioning as usual. If anything, it's veered off on another course that is totally unplanned and unmanaged. The decisions most likely to be left unmade are the very ones you are most interested in; promotions and salary increases beyond the average increase. You are up against a situation in which much greater productivity, better ideas, all of the usual business advantages, can't be rewarded without risk of upsetting the organization's desirability as a merger partner. Hence, your career is put on the back burner.

Many merger consultants will advise top management to try to lock in (sign employment contracts with) key people. These people are unlikely to sign until they are sure who the new partner will be and which of the partner companies will ultimately have control. Sometimes both sides are stalling to improve negotiating positions and everyone else is busily looking elsewhere. Merger consultants may be financial whizzes, but few have much feeling for the internal politics of clients.

A merger can bring out the pruning instincts in management. In owner/founder companies this is an ideal time to get rid of all the people the owner never had the nerve to get rid of before. Until the idea of a merger struck, the owner was perfectly content to be his or her own power center. He or she loved to show off that power by keeping on people who could, and probably should, have been fired. Now, with the situation in transition it's important to strengthen the structure. Getting rid of the deadwood gives the organization a fine businesslike gloss. "We run lean here," the owner/founder says.

The merger may bring out a tremendous ambivalence in top management. It may expose the basic division within the ranks that precipitated the idea of a merger in the first place. It may make the owner conscious of his or her desire to do other things and reduce work time and responsibility. If the owner has included family as stockholders, it may show a congenital inability of the family to work together.

As you can see, the individual's career needs are far down the list. It isn't just that people are unreceptive to negotiating, they are positively unconscious. It's up to you to bring attention back to your career and focus your boss on what's in it for him or her to help you.

One thing that may help you is that there may be more openings. Some won't be filled as people leave on the theory that running lean will make the company more attractive. Some might be filled if anyone put his or her head up long enough to look around and get an overview. In your spot, that person must be you. If you are not plugged in at many levels so that you can pick up every vibration, you'll be a loser. You need to know not only who has left but who is seriously thinking of leaving. If you can see where vacancies are likely to occur, you'll have a much better chance of making a pitch for the job.

Don't forget that your interests and the organization's are not identical in this situation. You want to hang on until you can move or until you see that you must move. The organization's agenda is making itself as attractive to outsiders as possible. If this involves sorcery so be it. Don't let yourself be too much influenced by the general mood of caution. The people in management who've never been through a major power change are trying to find some direction. They can still make decisions. It's how much power they have that they aren't sure of.

The crux of the matter is this. In a merger situation no one, including the owner, is sure how much power he or she has. The fear is that any one decision could reduce the company's attractiveness or bargaining position. Therefore, it is better to do only the routine. This may never be discussed in your hearing or even by top management alone. That doesn't mean it is not the most important agenda item. It should dominate your strategy planning, your analysis, and the ways you choose to sell yourself.

Sell yourself as a convenience to management. You are more likely to get money if you can show that by taking over parts of several jobs you'll save the organization money; provide support for a beleagured management; and make the organization appear more rational. In most owner/founder companies, management organization reflects the tastes and the priorities of the owner/founder. That person may have preferred a "heavy" sales department but hired few accounting people because he or she disliked "bean counters." If you can make cogent arguments for a change in the structure that will make the company more attractive, you may get more money. This isn't only at the highest level of management. When companies are under scrutiny as merger partners, they are examined carefully for every wart and tick. You will also be learning some things you can sell to the merged company as well as to a new employer if that's necessary.

Mergers can go very quickly or they can take a year or so. Depending on the egos and the finances involved, you could have as much as two years to plan and implement your strategy. On the other hand, it would be much smarter to take no more than three months. As the merger approaches completion, there is a risk that people will decide that they should sit tight and do nothing. The more this philosophy surfaces, the more likely that you'll have to do the same. As soon as you hear rumors of a likely merger, you must take steps to get yourself in the strongest possible position. Your goals should include the following.

1. Find out what management really has in mind and within what time frame. If they are in the exploring/thinking stage you have some time to do the same. You will want to make contacts in any organization you hear mentioned as a possible partner. Look to your trade and professional associations for names.

2. Verify that your company is initiating this change rather than falling victim to a partner. If the company is likely to be eaten up, you will need different strategies. (See section three of this chapter.) The easiest way to do this is to see what the people in potential partner companies say.

3. Get as many job descriptions as you can and begin looking at those jobs whose occupants are likely to move early. If you have a written-out plan, you're likely to have some success in selling a harassed management trying to keep critical functions covered. You may even sell yourself into a higher level job than would be possible in calmer times.

4. Don't panic. Most crises are opportunities for the prepared. The reason people are victims is often that they sit in the road without a game plan. If you seem to be working to some purpose, you are safer than those who are spending all of their time on the politics of the rumor mill. You need to be plugged in, but it is not, and cannot be, a full time job.

The Reorganization with Fallen Idols

One Monday morning you come to your office and your boss isn't there. He or she has gone on to the corporate outplacement center, known internally as Andersonville. There is a very clean but empty office next to you. Even the plants are gone. This is the first inkling you have had that a very major housecleaning is under way.

You can expect that during the 1980s the higher you go, the

more you earn, the more likely you are to be meeting with out-placement specialists from time to time. There seems especially to be no job security at the CEO level. This is not all bad. It's far preferable to being fired with nothing but a few weeks severance pay. Actually the vanquished one is usually in better emotional shape than those who witness his or her removal. The witnesses are not getting any counseling to help them cope with the sense of being next or just a generalized sense of impending doom.

Any time there is a change in top and middle management that involves as much as 25 to 30 percent of the people, the effect on your career and your morale can be devastating unless you know what to expect and what to do. If you are prepared, it's an opportunity. If not, you're a victim.

There may or may not be a logical explanation for the upheaval. The most common reasons include declining profits, market share, or stock prices; changes in top management that will now try to bring in its own people; or fear of a major market upheaval. There may be no explanation except that the president or CEO believes it's time for a good shaking up. This may be a periodic cataclysm that occurs because there is a need to keep everybody working at top speed. If you haven't been through one before it is horrifying. Sometimes the changes have a domino effect with each level copying what's been done one level up.

You are in the most danger if you have been moved rapidly, or more rapidly than normal, by a boss who's among the missing. Marked with the sign of a fallen idol, you'll have to move quickly to establish your independence. If you have had a great deal of visibility, it will be difficult to convince people that you'll now fade into the woodwork. Don't try. You are always a possible target if your interests are too closely tied to someone who's been axed. It's better to face this and see what other opportunities are available. As in the first situation, some people will not want to stay around to see who else is on the hit list. Try to sniff out if anyone whose job you'd like is planning to take flight.

Ask questions. What is going on? You may get no answers but that in itself is revealing. Try to gauge the level of fear among your peers and superiors. Try to get enough information to make an educated guess as to how widespread the changes will be. It's unlikely that whatever has prompted this reorganization happened on a Friday evening and the reorganization began on Monday. That's why it's so important to be watching every minute.

Most people are more affected by the fear of change than the actual changes made. They will leave regardless of the economy. Many talented people will leave rather than adjust to a new boss's style. In some cases the new boss will want as many people as possible to leave so that he or she can bring in people with styles known to be compatible. To a boss who comes into your department you are a new employee. New means unknown, and you can be as attractive to an outsider as you decide it's worth your while to be. Don't assume that the new boss is automatically against you because you've been there. You may not be a threat if you seem willing to suspend your judgment on that boss until he or she can prove him or herself.

Look for opportunities to add new duties and to negotiate for more money at the same time. Prepare your proposals in writing and show why what you propose will help the new boss. Expect that most of the assignments you get now are interim ones until the new boss decides on a final or semipermanent structure. Don't be put off by the fact that you will probably have several jobs during the year or so that the new management will take to get things running smoothly. These are learning opportunities that would take years to duplicate anywhere else.

You wanted to stay here, remember? If you wanted one job, with no need for constant watchfulness and constant maneuvering, you would have moved to another, more stable organization. The rule you should follow is to always get a raise or some other monetary concession as you take on new duties or move from job to job. If you don't do this, you are not bettering yourself and will eventually be forced to move outside the company anyway.

In nonprofits the decision to reorganize tends to be more democratic, or to appear so. There are usually meetings of committees that do needs analyses, projections, etc. Try to serve on one of these or be plugged in at a level where you get regular progress reports. If you can pick up the direction the group is going or sense who's likely to emerge on top, you can plan how you'll sell yourself into a better job. The process will take much longer in nonprofits than in companies unless the nonprofit is under some serious financial pressure to shape up. The more pressure the nonprofit is under the more opportunity there is for you as people scramble to get jobs filled and departments restructured.

You will need to be unusually circumspect in your dealings with the rumor mill during this period. The fear people have that they will lose out, particularly in a nonprofit, heats up the political atmosphere to the point that some people are lashing out at anyone they fear may gain from the situation. Don't ever share your strategies or your assumptions about what's going on. Pass on verifiable rumors only. Your strategies must be secret from everyone until they are either implemented or discarded. If you don't keep these very quiet you'll find others who are copying you to your hurt.

When Bob began to work on the new boss for a promotion to assistant manager, he told a colleague that he saw himself as the likely candidate. "If I get this promotion it'll be an easy jump out of the department to a manager's job in another department," he said. To his surprise, his colleague passed that statement on to the boss as part of the colleague's own bid for the job. Loyalty, sometimes a factor in shaky situations, got the colleague the job and Bob into temporary purdah.

The Unfriendly Takeover with Management Resistance

One day the happy, cash rich company wakes up to find itself under siege. A large, hungrier company is looking it over in a most predatory fashion licking its lips. The wagons are circled and the war begins. Anyone who would so much as suggest that even an unfriendly takeover might be good for the company is in mortal danger. Management's single agenda is to resist the takeover and thereby insure their own jobs at whatever price.

Obviously you are going to have only two choices. Join the resistance movement or get out. If you join the resistance you'll be faced with some serious risks. Your initial strategy has been to stay with the company until you are able to move. With the organization under siege there is a chance that the other side will win. If you were a visible part of the resistance, your long-term future, say the day the new management takes over, is compromised. A second risk is that even if present management wins they may do so only because they make enough internal changes to keep the stockholders happy. Those changes may include getting rid of your division, department, or you. Don't ever assume that if you are invisible you're safe. As in a real shooting war, nobody is safe who's in the battle zone.

There are strategies for joining the resistance without increasing one's visibility to the danger point. Give support to your boss who, after all, still has primary control over your career. Adopt a wait-and-see attitude tinged with tolerance for how much suffering this crisis is causing management. Keep working at top speed and increase the amount of selling you do about your work through the grapevine.

Let your boss know that you're available for occasional extra duty if necessary. Begin learning the jobs of the people around you or at least try to find out what these are. There will always be attrition during an unfriendly takeover attempt as many people can't stand working in a crisis atmosphere for more than a few weeks. The casualties may provide opportunities for you. If you can secure a new job or add to your present job and get a raise, you'll be working much harder than usual. If you do well it may help you with the new management, assuming the takeover is successful.

Keep abreast of what the business press is saying about the takeover attempt. If they are pessimistic, try to find out why. Develop contacts in the takeover company. Remember that unless you're president of the company, a director, or major stockholder, it's not really your fight. The same with your counterparts in the takeover company. Learn as much as you can. Do they think the bid is likely to succeed? Most people in the takeover company are nearly unconscious of such machinations unless they are in top management in which case they are unlikely to talk. This information may help you with your boss. Yes, you are providing a spy service, but it's good for you to find out as much as you can anyway. Who else will protect your interests?

If you're really concerned about staying with your present company do a literature search of the business press on the takeover organization. What have they done after a takeover? How many people lost jobs outside of the top management ranks? Any bloodbaths at your level or just one level above? Did the takeover improve earnings? What departments or divisions were axed? These questions must concern you even if you're a secretary or run the mailroom and you want to stay where you are. If you can predict the probable time frame and course of action of the takeover company you'll know more about what your own strategy should be. Don't assume that as long as you are a team player you're safe. In any crisis situation, everything is at risk and every assumption should be questioned. As we move farther into the 1980s and more companies face obsolescence, increased foreign competition, and changing consumer tastes and lifestyles, the sharks will have a field day. Where do you fit in? You are the only one who can and will protect your interests. Knowledge is power in these situations. Question all assumptions, your own and everyone else's. You cannot know what people in the takeover company are thinking. Expect that the best minds in your own organization are trying to figure out what the opposition is going to do and they'll be lucky to be right half the time. Don't worry about fairness or rightness. This is business and the operative principle is the bottom line. If you keep telling yourself how unfair the takeover attempt is, you'll simply divert your energy from the main event, which is protecting your interests.

The more upbeat your attitude and behavior the more likely you are to influence others to help you. The tendency to funereal responses is great and the contrast in your attitude and behavior may encourage others.

A Change in Company Philosophy, Direction, or Product Line

All of the sudden people no longer want presweetened cereals or gourmet canned peas. They're buying natural foods and generics and not much else. In a few months it occurs to management that their old act isn't selling in the hustings, and if they want to keep the company profitable, they'd better make some changes.

A nonprofit could arrive at the same spot in the road when it realizes that its clients no longer want or will accept the kind of help it's designed to provide and that some changes must be made quickly. For instance, after the March of Dimes helped with the development of polio vaccine it's major reason for existence ceased to be. It needed a new cause or all of those administrators would be unemployed. The field of birth defects was open and a switch was made.

In companies the initial signal that a change must be made usually comes from a decline in sales. If it's a precipitous decline, it may be a reflection of the economy, but a gradual, steady decline usually means a far more serious problem.

From your point of view, far removed from the department that is sweating over the ailing product or service, the problem is the company's loss of confidence and direction. While management scrambles to sort out its possibilities, everything else is put on hold. Raises tend to disappear even if the company overall is still profitable as every dollar is going toward bringing the sick division back. Since there is always the possibility that the division won't come back, it's important for you to see what opportunities you have internally.

The crisis shares one thing with the other three previously described. Those people with a low tolerance for change and uncertainty will begin to bail out. They will do this despite a shaky economy, pension considerations, and a genuine allergy to job hunting. You can do fine in this situation in terms of finding a new job or creating one internally if you keep two things in mind.

Management may not have a clear fix on what the market wants. It may try things that make the company poorer and weaker. If you allow the fact that you see this going on around you to frighten you, you'll end up spending all of your time on defensive, not offensive, strategies. Only boldness will get you more money in this situation. There is simply no way to lash yourself to a sinking ship and make more money doing it. If you act independently, rather than react, you'll be in much better shape to take advantage of any internal opportunities.

Keep up your outside contacts and expand them. You must spend some of your evenings and lunch hours at all of those association meetings you've been avoiding. This kind of crisis is the most unpredictable and therefore most dangerous. If management has lost its sense of mission or direction, the company could go into bankruptcy, merge, be taken over, or simply close its doors. Unless you keep your contacts honed, you might have trouble moving very quickly should the need arise.

Sometimes top management in a company is collectively seized with the need to try a new product or new direction. In the most extreme form of this disease they simply abandon all else and work on the new idea. If this happens what you are witnessing is the formation of a new business, not cosmetic surgery on the old. Treat this situation as you would an initial job hunt. While your boss knows you and what you can do, you are going to have to sell him or her on how your talents fit into the new scheme. That means keeping abreast of everything that's passing through the rumor mill. Otherwise you won't have any idea as to what you're selling, or should be.

This is probably the longest running crisis. New products or services don't spring full-blown from the brains of research and development teams. It can take five years to develop something which has even a remote chance of viability. Therefore you'll have more thinking, planning, and selling time. Do not allow your efforts to lag, however, because you seem to have more time. The road from idea to product is covered with checkpoints at any of which management may abandon the enterprise.

There is also greater risk that management may not have made a firm commitment to the new, but is using it as window dressing. In this case they may cease efforts in a particular direction at any time. This means that the situation is *permanently* unstable. If you are looking for stability, this is not your arena.

A Gradual or Precipitous Decline in Profits

The books are closed at the end of the quarter and to your amazement, if not to everyone else's, the company lost money. It's actually wading quite deeply in red ink. The stockholders, used to modest, dependable quarterly dividends are screaming for blood. They'll get it, too; usually through the sacrifice of one of the top corporate officers. It might be the chairman of the board if the situation is serious enough and other directors sufficiently alarmed.

The initial reaction from top management is to cut everything to the bone. Every single expense and salary that anyone can show might be surplus is cut, including many that aren't. An orgy of cost cutting begins regardless of the reason for the unprofitability. This gives stockholders, bankers, and the board of directors the feeling that something is being done. Whether this will help the profit picture or further weaken the company is immaterial. Movement equals progress. In such situations only bottom line arguments mean anything.

Your strategy is to show why paying you more and restructuring your job will generate savings and improve productivity. Any other argument is likely to go unheeded as everyone looks for some tangible evidence that nothing is being wasted, and war is being waged on the problem. If the company operates on a line item budget, that is, so much for salaries, so much for overhead, so much for supplies, etc., it's easier to sell a raise when it's part of a general restructuring than when it stands out in contrast to a general austerity program.

Other companies are watching yours. They may think that while the company is sound and just having a temporary downturn, this would be an ideal time to attack. This may mean increased marketing efforts by competitors, raids for key people, or a takeover attempt. Any of these will further unsettle your management. In many ways, this is the most dangerous situation of the five for you. You can be cut in a minute, not because you're unproductive or surplus, but because a certain percentage of salaries must be saved and yours is among them.

This aggressive uncertainty means that you'll have to be reducing your personal expenditures, building yourself up financially, and otherwise preparing for the worst. In no other situation are events as likely to move so quickly.

By now you can see that in any of these situations the key is to act boldly, not react in fear. So many other people will be cowering that your actions will be a favorable contrast. The bottom line is that nothing, particularly invisibility, will protect you anyway. Don't even consider head-in-the-sand as a strategy. If the company goes under or changes radically, you may be among those washed out. Since everything you do is high risk anyway, you'd be much better off to decide which of the high-risk alternatives is the least high risk for you. There are no safe strategies for top management nor you either.

The final do's and don'ts for all five crises include the following.

1. *Do improve your performance and merchandise the improvements.* Regardless of how effective you have been in the past, rev yourself up. It's always a temptation for new management to retain the top producers even if they were on the losing side. Also it will help you move on if you must.

2. *Do mend your political fences with everyone.* If you've offended anyone, clear up the difficulty. You can't afford a single enemy. In fluid situations, how can you predict who will survive?

3. *Do keep your mouth shut.* You are more likely to be done in by your own tongue than by a competitor or predator. The grapevine during a crisis is so sensitive that if you raise an eyebrow it will reverberate through the entire company. For example, one innocent remark expressing a soupçon of doubt about top management's survival made to a mailroom clerk could get you called on the carpet. Everyone is nervously examining every bit of information for meaning beyond the words. Did your remark mean that you knew something? Does it mean the troops are getting ready to abandon ship? It's a tiny step from there to seeing you as a bad influence on morale.

4. *Don't abandon your strategy because of one setback.* You will have no strategy at all if you keep changing it substantially every time you hear a new rumor. Try to verify everything you hear with at least two sources. The principal danger in these crises is that people will strike out without any thought of consequences. If you keep shifting from one strategy to another, it will be difficult to assess what works. You won't be able to duplicate anything that is successful.

5. *Don't let down your guard.* You can have no firm alliances with your peers, superiors, or subordinates in a fluid situation. Each of those people must act in his or her own self-interest no matter what he or she may have promised you. It's up to each

individual to secure a paycheck. If you take personally the defection of people you considered friends, you'll be emotionally hurt when you most need all of your emotional strength.

6. *Above all, don't let yourself be unemployed with no health insurance.* At the first sign of a crisis it's important to find out from personnel what the provisions are for carrying the policy yourself even if only temporarily. It will be very expensive to do so but it's absolutely necessary.

There may come a time at which the need to change jobs far outweighs any advantages of staying where you are. If you have been keeping up your outside contacts, this can be a fairly painless transition. Depending on your level in the organization you may be laid off rather than leave if the layoff includes some severance pay. Don't stay until you're laid off with only current salary.

The best research we've been able to gather suggests that you have about a one in two chance of surviving a major upheaval. This is an average and like any average not helpful in any one particular case. Obviously if the company goes under, no one survives, while in other cases 90 percent may be there after all of the changes are made. It's difficult to tell in advance. Your job will be to make sure that you do everything possible to protect your career.

10

The Reentry
Woman

Two days before her 42nd birthday Norma's husband announced his immediate intention to decamp from their suburban home in favor of a new life downtown with a 30-year-old lawyer. He pointed out that Norma's presidency of the Junior League did not, in his opinion, constitute a serious career despite the fact that it may have been fulfilling. "Everybody knows that housework and volunteer work retard a woman mentally," he announced. With those words of wisdom he left the name of his divorce lawyer and departed.

In looking at her life at that point, Norma saw three things clearly. She would have to get a job that paid her a decent wage and quickly. Alimony was nothing she'd want to count on, particularly if her husband decided to wed his new love and start a second family. Even if he were generous in his child support, her standard of living would soon be more dependent on her than on him. Second, her social standing was going to change radically. No more Noah's ark, her married friends would see her as an extra, even an undesirable extra. She was going to be a new and possibly permanent member of the formerly married, or as one of the singles groups in town put it, the "second-time singles." Third, she had, so far as she could see, no job skills that would vault her into middle management in a matter of weeks or months. She had not worked outside the home since college, twenty years ago. Her volunteer work was more prestigious than immediately marketable.

Norma fortunately had both a tremendous rage and desire to show her husband his skunkly qualities and enough religion left not to shoot herself. Nothing in the first three months after The Event gave her the least encouragement and everywhere she went she was told that unless she typed well and took shorthand she was going to continue to meet with discouragement. Norma enrolled in typing and shorthand courses at the local junior college.

Norma is so typical she doesn't even excite surprise any more. The suburbs in any part of the country are loaded with Normas and Normas-to-be. In fact, one in two women over 40 can expect to spend time as a single regardless of the stability at present of her marriage. The abandoned housewife is no longer news and a much less sympathetic figure than the suddenly widowed though their job situations are often quite similar. Somehow many assume the housewife was enjoying a free ride and like all free rides this one had to end sooner or later.

The myth that every suburban housewife who's abandoned will get a generous settlement from a husband eager to dump her is dying a slow death. It simply isn't true. Most will find themselves moving down the social scale and facing perilous financial times. The most someone in Norma's position can hope for is enough child support to raise any children still at home. It may even be an extended legal scrimmage to get college money.

The reasons that marriages break up don't interest us nearly as much as what Norma, and all her suddenly single sisters, can and should do not simply about a job or career but about catching up financially and in terms of a career.

What Stops the Reentry Woman

Most reentry women have a crisis of confidence. This is despite and in spite of the media attention, the college courses, and the seminars conducted by consultants who've "been there." They simply don't believe they are now, or more importantly, can be competitive with their career sisters who've worked since college or whose careers were interrupted by only a 3- or 5-year absence from the job market. As a result they tend to act out this lack of confidence in every job-related situation. At the least, they are tentative in interviews and less likely to sell a prospective employer hard. As one woman said, "If I don't try anything too spectacular I won't scare myself to death. If I don't make any spectacular promises I won't have to worry about fulfilling any that I do make." Spectacular for her meant trying to turn her past experience, even though nonpaid, into a better than entry level job.

Reentry women expect their career sisters to shun them. Therefore, they are not terribly surprised when this prophecy is self-fulfilling. They share in their reentry networks each story about the woman who interviews them, herself a genuine career woman, then seems to devalue life or volunteer experience as opposed to on-the-job experience. They do not challenge this devaluation. They are sure that if they seek help from women who have always worked, they will be told where the bottom rung on the ladder is and pointed in that direction. Unfortunately this is not entirely myth. Many queen bees are also black widows. Women in their forties who've worked since high school or college may act out their hostility both to reentry women and to younger women who aren't or may not be forced into "paying their dues" as these women have had to by trying to keep them in their place, which is usually unemployed or unpromoted. A few rotten apples don't spoil the barrel, just themselves. They should be gotten around as there are plenty of others to whom sisterhood is more than a blood relationship.

Reentry women ask other reentry women for advice. Thereby they multiply their misinformation. Instead of hearing from people who have done the kinds of things necessary to move ahead quickly, they learn about techniques that haven't worked. One method that you learn works is worth more than twenty methods that didn't. Even if you discover twenty methods that don't work you still don't know one that does. People don't learn from mistakes nearly as much as they learn from successes.

Reentry women, especially those who were forcibly divorced, are already suffering from a massive case of rejection shock. Any hint of rejection in the job market (it's impossible to job hunt without being rejected a few times) is magnified many fold because of the state of mind of these women. Therefore, all refusals of employment are totally personal. "I am being rejected again as myself," the woman says. The absurdity of this never occurs to her because she never stops to think that a prospective employer doesn't know her well enough to reject her personally. That person is responding only to the outline of her that he or she sees.

The reentry woman has ambivalent feelings about how seriously she should pursue a career. She doesn't say to herself, "This is it. I am now a serious career person. Housewifery is behind me forever." First it isn't true. She'll always be at least a part time housekeeper doing the same tasks. Second, such a statement implies commitment and her instincts are against that. She grows into a career point of view if she ever adopts it. Keep in mind that this is true of women in general. Not every woman who appears to be a serious career woman is. Some have simply adopted protective coloration. Women who look and act as if they are serious move much more quickly or are thought to.

The reentry woman secretly nurses the hope that she'll work in a nice place where she'll meet a man her own age who'll take her away from all of this. She will wander in the corporate wilderness for a few years and then be magically returned to her chosen career as hostess and Nancy Reagan clone, though this time it may be a city condominium rather than the grass and trees of suburban BD (before divorce).

The bitter reenty woman who sees her entire life's work to date ridiculed by its chief beneficiary, her former spouse, may nurse her bitterness for a few months or several years, handicapping herself very seriously in the job hunt. She may not be aware of the degree of her bitterness and the harm she's inflicting on herself. Her more sympathetic friends may dismiss this as normal. It may be. It's also self-destructive and poverty inducing.

The reentry woman has bought into every myth about age. It does not impress her at all that Ray Kroc started MacDonald's when he was over 50 years old and had not succeeded at anything else very much until then. She is even less impressed with the late Colonel Harlan Sanders of Kentucky Fried Chicken fame, also a very late bloomer. She can see no parallels in their careers and her own. After all, they had presumably always been working. The career woman she's most familiar with, if at some distance, is the one her husband is alleged to have abandoned her for. She may make light of her age, but it is a prime agenda item. She will do a great many things solely to make herself look or feel younger.

The reentry woman cannot get over the unfairness of the blow she's been dealt. She worked so hard! She played the marriage game exactly by the rules in force when she got married. She played tennis, decorated the house, raised the children, signed up for aerobic dancing when it became fashionable, watched her weight and his, in short, she did everything possible to perfect housewifery. She feels richly entitled to compensation for the rejection she's suffered and becomes further embittered when her ex is not punished in court.

Crippled with at least some of these attitudes, the reentry woman needs to rethink her position before she begins a serious job hunt. She needs some strategy planning. She needs to look again at her assets instead of concentrating with such tenacity on her liabilities.

Norma didn't get much counseling because her suburb didn't have any programs for reentry women. The junior college where she'd enrolled for her typing and shorthand courses wasn't as interested in reentry women as in full-time students. With more help, Norma might have turned her volunteer work to greater effect. As it was, it took two years to find ways to package that information. Still, by instinct or trial and error Norma did a great many things right.

From the start Norma determined that she was going to catch up with her career sisters and move ahead just to get even with her former spouse. She committed herself fairly single-mindedly to that. In order to do so she needed to pursue some career for which her BA in English from Smith was adequate if not spectacular. No MBA at night for her, she simply didn't have the time or money. Her first principle, though she would hardly have expressed it as such, was that she was going to merchandise herself as someone running in the fast lane. She wasn't a beginner; in fact, she could never be a beginner again. She'd have to find a place that valued what she was, not what she was not and could never be, young and an MBA, for instance.

Norma bought the requisite business suits, prepared a sort of chronological resume, and began interviewing. Result: total failure. Her best job offer was as a receptionist for a large law firm in the central city. It paid $9500 per year. After taxes she would not be able to make her mortgage payment and eat in the same month even if she stuck to dry cereal and ate it in the dark and cold. She began to think of selling the house. In three months, she sold the house, shared the money with her husband under protest and bought a condominium in a far more modest neighborhood closer to a major industrial area.

Norma began to spend her evenings at women's groups and trade association meetings. Three months later she heard, through a friend, of a job in a small real estate development office. It was for a receptionist/typist/bookkeeper, and it paid $10,700 a year. It wasn't much but after looking for six months it was considerably better than nothing. She took it. Norma saw herself as someone that an employer would only take if no one else better or younger was available but fortunately her employer didn't share that view. He was delighted with Norma. She was so sensible and responsible. Everyday he congratulated himself on his astuteness in having rejected any number of 17-year-olds for this woman. He said this quite often to Norma and to other people in the office, which boosted her ego.

There wasn't really enough to do on the job and Norma began to watch what others were doing. She was always willing to help the secretaries with typing, collating, or running errands. They liked her and took her under their wings and taught her the shortcuts and a lot about office politics and managing the boss. She'd been there about eight months when a friend called and told her about a job as secretary in a small computer manufacturing firm. It paid $13,900. As much as Norma liked both her employer and her coworkers, she felt terribly pinched on the salary she received. She interviewed for the job and got it.

Norma worked very hard as a secretary for the computer firm and again the office was small enough so that people noticed. Her boss asked her to help out on the bookkeeping when the bookkeepeer was absent. She did and received a $1000 raise after she'd been there only three months. Two months later the bookkeeper left for greener pastures and Norma became the head bookkeeper with an assistant and got a raise to $16,500.

That helped but she still wasn't satisfied with the money. She decided that bookkeeping wasn't for her and took a couple of personnel courses at a local university. She thought of pursuing a Masters degree in industrial relations but faced the same obstacles faced with the MBA: no time, not enough money. The university encouraged her in this decision by announcing that she'd have to make up only six course deficiencies before she could begin the Masters program.

One year later the company expanded and hired six new people for the front office. Clearly they would now need an office manager. Norma marched into the boss and asked for the job. She gave all of the appropriate arguments as to why she'd be good, including her volunteer work, emphasizing especially her inside knowledge of the way the company liked things done. After some stalling, frantic looking and interviewing outside the company, the boss's resistance collapsed and Norma got the job. She negotiated (as in Chapter 4) for a base salary of $20,000 and a performance-based bonus at the end of each year. Her next goal is to negotiate a chance to buy some of the company's stock. She's convinced the stock is going to be worth a lot of money someday because the company is growing and does make a good product.

Norma's first bonus was $6,000 and by late 1980 she was earning a total of $28,000 a year, not bad for a woman who began her career in 1978 at $10,700. It gave her a lot of satisfaction to know that many *real* career women made about the same for the same work. Some even made less. If you were to meet Norma tomorrow, you would not mistake her for the role models you've seen in *Working Woman* or *Savvy.* She still has, despite her yards of gray flannel, a faint aura of a refugee from aerobic dancing classes and tennis lessons. She's still somewhat suburban. What you would notice, however, is how confident Norma is that she can do her job and take care of herself. If she does find another "Mr. Right," it's doubtful that she'll abandon her job for another crack at housewifery. She likes the new her too much.

What did Norma do that made her working life come together and turn into something resembling a good job that other women in the same circumstances can duplicate?

• *Norma understood that she didn't have time to wait to be recognized or to move up within an organization in the normal way.* A company that rewards longevity would be death for her. That automatically excluded many of the largest firms in her town. She couldn't afford to pay her dues. She had to find a place anxious for a competent hard working person regardless of her past. Norma interviewed with 15 large corporations before she realized that they didn't need her. They could have their pick of younger, admittedly better trained women, who wanted prestige and long-term opportunity more than they wanted money. Neither the real estate firm nor the computer firm had beautiful downtown offices near fine shops and restaurants. They both worked out of cramped, cheap offices with tacky furniture, which generally lacked the amenities. They wanted people who worked very hard and who saw money as the chief reward. Norma fit their image. These much smaller companies didn't want to train anybody. They didn't have time. They wanted to tell someone something once, safe in the knowledge that it would be done.

• *Norma ignored nonprofit organizations.* She recognized that a university, while prestigious and often picturesque and pleasant, was not for her. A hospital had a very rigid hierarchy and the doctors on top were loathe to share either power or money. Even though at this time she could not really articulate the relationship between power and money she knew instinctively that a place that tried to supplement inadequate pay with the prestige of working there was a luxury she could ill afford. She needed a fast track and in a stagflation no nonprofit could offer this.

• *Norma sold her past as a benefit.* She didn't try to conceal that she'd spent 20 years as a housewife and mother. She played on that. Finally she even told of the volunteer work she'd done, the responsibility she'd had. After so many tries at making what she'd done seem more important than most employers could understand she decided to be totally honest. She said, "I need this job. I'll work hard and produce for the company. Give me a chance." It was an irresistible pitch for the real estate developer who'd already been through five 17-year-olds who were simply marking time in his office while waiting for Saturday night.

• *Norma sold her age as a benefit.* Not everyone is enamoured with youth despite the media impression. Norma decided that there wasn't much she could do about being 43. She might look 35, but she was still 43. She might as well sell it as a plus. She pointed out that she had a great deal of stability and was seriously committed to making something of her career, which at this point was still more theory than fact. She pointed out that she'd be unlikely to leave for pregnancy or to follow a man across the country. She'd always been dependable. That was something one could not always say about many younger people of either sex.

• *Norma realized that the so-called rules didn't work for her and that they didn't apply to her.* Getting an MBA at 42 wouldn't necessarily get Norma a job as a commercial loan officer for the largest bank in town. If she returned to school, finished her accounting courses, and passed the CPA examination she wouldn't be hired by a large public accounting firm and placed on the fast track to partnership.

Norma saw that if she job hopped to move up quickly, it wouldn't be the same kind of liability for her it would be for a woman in her thirties, with 10 years experience. She could do that for the first few jobs. In fact, if she expected to double her salary in a short period of time, that was the principal way she could do it.

• *Because of her age Norma realized she had to be far more careful with and about money.* Norma's attitudes toward money had to undergo a radical change. She now had less of it and would have less for at least the first five to eight years of her career than she did at the time her marriage ended. Unless she adjusted both her thinking and her standard of living, she was going to face financial trouble and anxiety on a scale she had never dreamed. Norma was positively bright in deciding to sell her home once the burden of making the payments fell on her. Even if she'd had four children at home, she could have found cheaper housing. Selling her home was the symbolic step in adjusting to her new life. With all of the reentry women we've seen, that was the crucial step. If they could not give up this vestige of their old status and life, not to mention nonworking neighbors, they were not ready to pursue a career with the singlemindedness that was necessary to launch them.

Norma had to learn to value what she earned because she had earned it, rather than mourn the past. This was probably the most difficult transition. It meant giving up the unrestricted use of credit cards, both developing and following a budget, and never letting her standard of living quite match her earnings. Norma also learned that she had to do her own financial planning: no more 5½ percent savings accounts for her! She'd starve in her old age if she didn't make some plans. She got the facts on as many pension plans as possible and decided to start an IRA and shelter some of her income. She wanted to control her own future. She could put that money into stocks and manage it as she saw fit. In contrast, she could not plan to move from company to company if each company had a retirement plan. She'd never be fully vested in any one of them unless she stayed at one for 10 years, which would not have met her income goals.

Norma's way was one useful strategy but by no means the only strategy. What propelled Norma was her strong desire for security, self-generated security. She was determined to take care of herself. That need is not as strong in everyone. Many women are pursuing a different kind of security in a different way.

When Joan's husband died, she was 36. She had three children under 12, a four-bedroom house in a suburb so far from the central city as to be light years away, and barely enough life insurance to bury her husband properly. When she started on her job search, it occurred to her immediately that a woman with no work experience, an acute child care problem, and only three years of college would have a problem. Eventually, she chose the same route that Norma took with one variation. Having decided that even getting a job interview would be difficult, she began immediately to go to as many professional group meetings as she could and talk to as many people working for large companies as she could. Her greatest need, she felt, was a company with superb medical benefits and life insurance. She needed a special kind of large company, however. She couldn't have one that wouldn't so much as talk to a non-college graduate or one that valued seniority above everything. What she eventually decided on was on a medical supply company that was starting a word processing department.

Joan knew very little about word processing except that it was supposed to be a growth area. However, one of the women she met at a networking group told her that her company was gearing up and hiring people for a brand new word processing department. No experience was required, not even typing, as word processing was something for which the workers would be trained. Joan knew that this was not the key to the executive washroom but it was a ground floor opportunity. She went for the interview, arranged by her contact, and got a job.

Joan decided that to apply herself here was as good a place to start as any. The job was not particularly difficult. It was repetitive, and the most interesting thing was that the equipment was constantly changing. She began work at $9,800 a year with a review in three months. At the first review she told her supervisor that if any of the others were having trouble with the equipment she'd be glad to help out. The supervisor, busy with relationships with users and the normal shake-out of a new installation, welcomed Joan's offer. Within another month the supervisor had turned over most of the follow-up training to

Joan. The initial training was done by the manufacturer's people who, identifying Joan as the person likely to be most useful to them, tried to give her more information. They took her to lunch when they were at the company and generally made her feel that she was on the right track.

The supervisor, far from jealous of the attention Joan received, saw her as a godsend. She encouraged Joan's growing expertise and helped her get a 15 percent raise at the end of nine months. Part of the reason was that the supervisor was grooming Joan as her replacement. She realized that Joan could handle the job and that having a replacement in the wings would enable her to move on. Ambitious on her own behalf, the supervisor wanted to move to a much bigger installation and was always angling for such an opportunity through her contacts at the local branch of the word processing association. Joan went to the meetings as well, as both of them found interesting people and ideas there.

One year after Joan started at the company, her supervisor announced her departure for a money center bank with a department of 100 people. Joan was heir apparent for supervisor. Since her salary had been raised twice in the first year, the company balked at another large increase. They felt that she was moving ahead too quickly and that it might encourage others to expect large increases. Joan decided that while she wanted the supervisor's job, she had to have the money. She began to do the kind of salary research outlined in Chapter 3. She found out that word processing supervisors for installations the size of her company's were paid at least $18,000 and more often $20,000 to $24,000 almost everywhere in town. She decided to put this together in a proposal for her boss. She laid out her information on a table showing the name of the company, the size of the department, the length of time it had been in operation, the salary of the supervisor, and the average salary of the operators. Since she'd gotten the information not from the company's personnel department but from supervisors themselves she had confidence in her facts.

Her boss was naturally surprised that Joan had prepared herself so thoroughly. She pointed out three reasons that the company should pay her market price for her work, but she got agreement on each point before she went on to the next.

1. If they hired a supervisor from outside they would have to pay at the high end of the range. That person would then still have to learn how the users in this company liked the work done. There would be a period of learning about this company's equipment and people that would add to the company's costs before the new person could be productive.

2. Joan wanted to make a career with this company. Unlike the old supervisor she wanted and needed the stability of a steady job and the excellent medical coverage provided by the organization.

3. The company already had a significant investment in Joan. The departing supervisor, wise to the ways of corporate politics, had made sure that Joan was the only one capable of taking over the department. This was not so much her strong support of Joan as her realization that none of the other women was the least bit interested in the job. *Note:* The supervisor did not actually *know* that the others were not interested, only that none appeared interested. She also realized that if she left the organization with a new department and no trained successor she risked damage to her reference.

After some agonizing and a great deal of concern about Joan's credentials (could the company promote a woman without a college degree regardless of her capability?) Joan got the job. She and the boss compromised on salary. She agreed to $17,200, and he agreed to six months' performance review and raise at that time of at least 12 percent, which itself was a compromise between 10 and 15.

Joan's goal is to stay with the word processing department and try to expand it physically and in influence over the next few years while she finishes her degree. For her, the MBA *is* an option if she's to get into managing a very technical area such as a combination of data processing and word processing. It's not that Joan couldn't be won away by a much better job in another company with similar benefits, but at this time the stability of staying one place for some years is important to her.

Joan's strategy was, and is, to create every opportunity that she can. She is not waiting to be chosen because she understands only too well that her own mobility depends as much on what she initiates as on anything the company sees fit to do for her. Joan sees herself as a saleswoman selling herself at every turn. She will be much more active internally because she has kept herself aware of events that may affect her department.

Finally, Joan is not likely to see her present job as permanent so much as she sees the company as potentially permanent. She's made a wise choice in a company that's growing at a rate one and one-half times the rate of inflation. The same job in a company that was not growing would have far fewer opportunities for her to move internally.

Even though Joan returned to college and finished her BA, she already learned something which is probably more valuable: how to negotiate with someone after she's got the information she needs. That skill will prove far more valuable than any she's likely to get out of her formal education because it is the one she'll use most often.

Both Joan and Norma learned about negotiating by doing it. Their need to do it gave each a kind of desperate courage. Those whose need is not as great, or who don't think it's as great, should still prepare themselves for negotiation. It is the one skill any reentry woman must have to move into an organization, much less ahead. See Chapter 5 again. It's critical for you.

Help for the Truly Fainthearted

Suppose that after reading this far you realize that both Norma and Joan are positively gutsy compared to you. What you'd like, what you fantasize about is someone coming to your home to offer you a job or a boss recognizing your sterling qualities and offering you a raise without your having to ask. You are living in a dream because the odds are heavily against you. There are things you can do right now, however, to help become more comfortable in the whole process of reentry and negotiation. Remember that the investment in time and pain needed to help you become more businesslike is a lifetime investment.

• *Sit down and write out what you want or need to earn on your next job or the percentage raise you want in your present job.* If you don't have enough information to do this, contact the professional association in your area. There is one which serves people like you. Start your search for this group in the Yellow Pages. For instance, if you're a secretary there is the National Secretaries Association. If you're in banking there's the National Association of Bank Women. If you're in some branch of communications there is Women in Communications, Inc. Overall there are something like 25,000 separate organizations, some for women only, others mixed. One of them can help you. Most are national and they will have a local group in or near where you live. If not, get information about the national headquarters from the Gale's Encyclopedia of Associations and write to them.

You will benefit in three ways from ongoing contact with an association.

1. You will find out what other people who have similar jobs actually do at work and how much they expect to be paid. There is no reliable source of this information other than people working at a particular job. This is especially important to reentry women who, contrary to popular belief, generally woefully underprice themselves. You don't ever have to ask someone directly what he or she makes. You can ask what someone doing a particular kind of job, which you describe in some detail, would make in that company.

2. Since the people you meet at association meetings are not direct competitors you can discreetly test your ideas on them.

They can and will share what has worked for them in the past. You will not believe how much more confident you'll feel when you find out that someone who's been working 10 or 15 years sweats when she must confront a boss. If she's successful, it's because she's learned to make that fear work for her. She can help you learn that too. It's not difficult to get people talking if you just say, "what do you do?"

3. You will have an ongoing source of job leads which occur from the natural movements from job to job of the members of these associations. This will reduce your level of anxiety. You will not face the prospect of "cold" calling on employers because you don't know of any leads when you need or want a new job. You will not be an outsider any more. Face it, for most reentry women the feeling of being different and a stranger to a new world is hateful and depressing.

• *You may want to practice your pitch to a boss or prospective employer in front of a mirror first.* Then practice with another person over and over before you talk to your boss. This seems so simple, but very few people do it. There is no substitute for knowing how someone will react or can react to what you are going to say. This technique will strengthen even the most faint-hearted especially if you practice with someone who's fairly critical and can ask tough, spur-of-the-moment questions.

• *Research the timing of your approach to a boss or prospective employer.* Monday morning, when you may be revved up and ready to go, is the worst time to approach many people. Friday afternoons is one of the best times. If you're a morning person pick a Wednesday morning. Most people have solved the previous week's crises by then and are simply working on routine things while waiting for new crises to develop. This is sometimes known as the midweek lull. Most people are situationally receptive. Your job is to plan the best time. Sometimes this means making an appointment. Other times it's being prepared to act when someone seems to be receptive or when the topic you want to talk about turns up unbidden in the conversation.

• *The most important idea you need to keep in mind about negotiating with a boss or prospect is that if she or he seems about to say no to whatever you've asked, try to postpone the rest of the conversation.* It's harder to change a *no* to a *yes* than a noncommittal or maybe to a *yes*. If what you've prepared isn't working, don't play out the hand. Retreat, rethink your position, and reapproach the person. For example, when Joan was negotiating her raise and promotion to her word processing supervisor, she never forced the issue with the boss. She never suggested that he must decide today or this week or she'd leave or lose interest in the job. Hers was a gentle pressure. She kept reiterating her points and talking about her research but never put the boss in the spot of having to agree or disagree overall. On specific points she would get agreement. She got the boss to agree that she was the most likely candidate and that she'd had enough training by her immediate boss to likely work out. She never nudged the boss into making a final choice until she felt confident of victory. The worst thing that can happen to a nervous negotiator is to become so uncomfortable that any decision, including *no,* is better than the uncertainty of not knowing.

• *If the idea of negotiation unsettles you, save your money and take a college course or a two-day seminar.* This is an investment in your future you can't afford not to make. Under no circumstances should you sign up for any course unless you can find and interview at least three people who've been through it. Ask the sponsoring institution or seminar leader for references. You can't afford to blow your time and money on slick advertising that has no substance.

• *Packaging is everything.* In fact, once you learn the theory of negotiation you'll still be constantly experimenting with how you package your message. Put a good chunk of your preparation time into thinking of different ways to say things. You may want to look at Chapter 6 on word games. In addition to what we've suggested, it would help you to write your own dialogue. Remember that you'll be negotiating under stress. That's why advance preparation is so important.

• *If one technique doesn't work try a different one.* There is no one method that will help you move quickly. There is, however, one or more techniques that will work more than half the time with one boss. These are the ones you're looking for.

• *The lower the rung on the ladder where you begin the more important negotiation is.* When you have no power to command, not even to decide when you'll be able to go to lunch for instance, you must rely on negotiation. If you don't try to negotiate, your working life will be completely dictated by others. You will be locked in to a way of doing things that may be entirely uncomfortable for you.

• *Keep notes on everything you try.* If you try negotiating for a raise and you get half as much money as you'd asked for, analyze why that happened. Didn't you ask for enough money in the first place? Does this particular boss always halve requests? Is there a company policy on percentages that this boss won't or perhaps can't violate? Don't simply treat a failure as a bad experience. You must try to analyze what did happen and how you might have turned it around.

• *Ask other people for their success stories.* Ask at meetings, cocktail parties, all kinds of social occasions. No one resists the opportunity of telling about his or her successes and you're learning what does work. What someone thinks might work for someone else isn't as important or useful as what did work for this particular person at one time. Knowing that a tactic you propose to try has worked in the past can give you courage. It's always more difficult to try things which seem to you totally untried. That requires a higher level of courage than many of us have.

• *Subject every strategy to the test of "what-do-I-have-to-lose."* It's unlikely you'll be fired for trying to better your situation. The greatest risk is that you'll be told no and feel uncomfortable or embarrassed. Still, consider the alternatives. If you don't try, you will always be dependent on the generosity and spirit of fairness of others. In good times this is often a vain hope. To count on this in hard times is not bright. You must help yourself if anyone is to take an interest in your problems.

As the number of reentry women continues to grow, as programs serving this special group become more useful, the problem of reentry above the bottom rung will diminish. Until then, it's important to get as much information as you can and to expect to do more than someone not in that situation might have to do.

11

Finding the Small Organization—Why Less Is Often More

Somewhere in your city there are numerous small businesses happily making money, sharing the wealth with their employees, and generally providing a variety of experiences and opportunities. They are almost totally invisible. They lack the drama in their workday lives or the magic name that would invite press coverage. Some are engaged in hot/hot fields laying the foundation for growth to challenge *Fortune* "500" leaders in five or ten years. Others are built around the ideas of one person who has decided to gamble on public acceptance of a particular product or service and is winning. Still others are spinoffs of larger companies. Now this fledgling is giving its former parent a run for money and markets.

When small businesses are mentioned, a great many otherwise astute career planners and salary maximizers yawn. They can't imagine that the action in a small company would be as good as it is in a larger one. They secretly value the glamour and prestige of a company the mere mention of whose name causes friends to say, "Wow!"

Most security minded people disdain small, new companies

because they fear two things. They worry that the small company will be family owned and overrun with nepotism. Surely there is nothing more discouraging than having to work with and for incompetents who you recognize would be on welfare save for the family business. If charity begins at home anyone who's ever worked in a family business would heartily endorse the sentiment that it should be kept there as well.

The second fear is that whatever management is doing is only temporarily successful, not something that will last over time. The feeling of insecurity is real. Even if the company's prospects are terrific by every rational measure, the fear of instability lurks in the background. A company that has a 40, 50, 100 year track record seems to proclaim its future longevity with its past. Even as people read about Chrysler and its soul brothers, they retain the impression that if you have done it for a long time, you have done it profitably. It's very difficult to fight gut responses with logic. One hears reports that only a tiny percentage of small businesses survive five years, much less grow and prosper to become industry leaders. The small business looks like a gamble—something for the fainthearted and security-oriented to avoid. Before you make such a short-sighted decision, you may want to think carefully about the advantages and disadvantages of working for a small business. A small business, as we use it here, is essentially any business that meets the following criteria.

• *Fewer than 100 employees and gross income of $10 to $20 million.* Why these numbers? Once a company moves out of this range it begins to develop a greater degree of specialization and rigidity. For instance, at about 100 employees managers usually still hire their own people. Managers may give each other leads because a strong sense of territoriality hasn't had time to take root. The personnel person, if there is one, is primarily a record keeper and government report filer. He or she does not really get involved in bugging management about its people choices.

Managers set salaries according to whim and budgets, or how much they want a prospect. This is not all bad from your point of view because it allows you free reign to sell yourself. If the company gets much larger, it will bring in a compensation specialist who may decide that what is needed is a system. Once a system is in place, much of the freedom may be gone. At the least, a system supplies management an excuse for turning you down. This is good if you are a plodder who can't face hard salary negotiation, and bad if you are trying to maximize your salary.

You will hear personnel people say that the company they work for is "run like a small business." Nothing but a small business can be run like a small business because while that may be management's intent, the rules change. Government at every level treats businesses differently according to size. Some regulations that small companies can ignore are mandatory for large ones. This cannot help but affect management style.

As Bill found when he moved from a huge manufacturing conglomerate to an owner/founder company in the same industry, the products were roughly the same, but the style and organization were vastly different. He was much closer to every decision the organization made and almost every day the owner and he crossed paths in the plant. Decision making could be seen; it was never done at a distance and passed down. The pace was considerably quicker as the owner looked over the problem and gave his opinion.

• *The company has been in business less than ten years.* If the company is long established, even though small, it will have developed some policies and ways of doing things that may be no less rigid than those of much larger companies. You are looking for new as well as small. The sense of excitement and adventure should still be there. This means you can expect some willingness to take risks and experiment. One of the risks may be hiring you. Once the organization finds the formula, it falls into the same bad habits as many larger companies. It refuses to change until there is a clear danger.

• *The company is growing at a rate at least one and one-half times the rate of inflation.* There is no point in even considering a small company that isn't booming. Why deal with stagnation and some instability at the same time? If you are taking risks, it should be on something that has much better than average prospects for growth and survival.

Let's look at some of the advantages of working for a small company; then some of the disadvantages; and finally, we'll examine how to find likely prospects.

The advantages include the following:

• *Fewer layers of management.* In a company with only two layers between you and the owner it's much harder for your superior to pass the buck. If you're constantly running into the owner or president in the lunchroom or at company functions, your ability to bring yourself to the attention of the ultimate power is much greater. You can get much closer to the power source. If you are viewed as a comer, when an opening appears you are automatically considered if it's something you can do. Many owners have a paternalistic attitude which makes them more responsive to the people already working at the company rather than wanting to look outside at every opportunity. You become more than a name and face and can be seen as a whole person. You are visible.

• *If the company does well, money is more likely to be distributed as bonuses or profit sharing.* It's much harder to hide prosperity from the rank and file in a small company because even the bookkeeper talks. Furthermore, it's only an extension of paternalism to share the wealth. It gives some owners a kick to tell others how much money their people made during a year. This makes them think they are good "providers." Owners understand that employees have hidden concerns about stability. They see cash as a way to combat these fears.

What Ann liked best about the small drug manufacturer was that every Christmas everyone, right down to the mail clerk, got a minimum of $1,000 as a bonus. After she'd been there five years she was earning $20,000 in salary and $7,500 as a bonus. She felt that the extra cash in one lump sum helped her invest the money instead of use it for a series of small, impulse purchases. In lean years, she received $3,400 so that even though she could not know the exact amount until the end of the year she could count on something extra. The fact that the amount couldn't be determined in advance was an added incentive to use the money for investment only. One of her investments was her IRA.

• *A real, as opposed to artificially created, team spirit exists.* Small companies frequently have an atmosphere in which the people are having fun. They love the process of building. The other side is that if the company stops growing or hits a temporary roadblock, these people are rapidly disenchanted. However, when the company is growing it's a delightful work environment because of the spirit of cooperation and adventure.

• *Management is not as concerned with how companies like this are managed.* There is something almost joyous in working for managers who have confidence in their own judgment and aren't always reading up to see if they are doing it right. Even if they make a mistake, it's not a tragedy because each has a solid core of belief in his or her own rightness. This is more likely to occur in a small business because there is less competition between managers of like departments. There is one marketing manager, not ten, each looking to see what every other one is doing.

While small companies do participate in trade and professional associations they see themselves as there to learn rather than to compare individual performance with an artificial standard. Life without the tyranny of the latest management theory is often twice as productive and supremely comfortable. Imagine the joys of never attending another Management By

Objective meeting or another three-day institute on Japanese style productivity. If you've been in an organization harassed by the latest management fad you might find a small business considerably more rational. You also may find people who don't consider an MBA from a top school (or any school) desirable, much less necessary.

• *Age discrimination is less likely.* You're 50 years old and look every day of it. You might even look older. In a small company you are more likely to be hired anyway because there is no pension plan and you will therefore not affect the numbers. You may have to pay for your own health insurance and life insurance, but no one will *not* hire you because you might *spoil* the group. You can be looked on as an individual because the company doesn't want to train the very young anyway. Youth is no advantage because corporate immortality and its pursuit aren't issues. The company is thinking about next year, not founder's day 90 years from now.

• *Your warts can be neutral or even assets.* With 50 employees, your individuality, however expressed, can be tolerated. Top management doesn't know that it's supposed to hire everyone with the same background, all graduated by the same university, with identical values. Many entrepreneurs are rather eccentric and therefore may be more tolerant of the eccentricities of others. While IBM may worship at the white shirt altar, a small company may not have a dress code, real or hidden. You may get away with your beard, 1960s mini skirts, 200 extra pounds, or whatever your failing or choice. True, small companies can be as rigid as large ones, but it's not as likely simply because a lot of entrepreneurs left big companies and started their own to get away from the conformity. They are less likely to impose it in the new situation.

• *You can argue for your ideas with greater freedom.* Small businesses tend to be more fluid and pragmatic as they are growing and allow for a greater expression of ideas. If it works, or seems logical and might work, it's worth considering. If you keep bugging top management with a crazy notion, it may be as bad for your career there as it would be any other place. If, however, you have valuable ideas to contribute, you'll find fewer layers between you and those who can help you turn your ideas into reality. The atmosphere may be more open than in a company which is formed of departments run by sheiks anxious to protect their individual sheikdoms.

• *Schedules for raises and promotions are less clearly defined.* This allows individual managers to make such decisions as they see fit. If you see your boss about a three months' increase, no one from personnel is likely to come around and nag him or her about a violation of company policy. There may not even be a policy. You can get what you can sell. Obviously this means you will need some highly developed negotiation skills.

• *You have more opportunities to teach yourself new skills.* There is no training department that has defined what is to be learned about a specific job. Each manager does on-the-job training as he or she sees fit or feels the need. If you can persuade your boss to let you try something new, you are essentially involved in self-training. If you want to learn something, you have only to sell the benefits of such knowledge to the company or to your boss. If you are using the small company as a proving ground or to help you maximize your salary and promotional opportunities in the shortest period of time, you'll find you can do this more easily because so much less structure is there to block you. No need to apply for an interdepartmental transfer, just sell the manager on taking you in.

• *Rapid growth creates more opportunities.* If you started in the sales department and the company suddenly needs or thinks it wants a sales promotion department, you may have a chance to move there if you are interested. After all, you are already on-site. It may be assigned to you to research the problem and find out what is best for the sales division and then implement it. Assignments are distributed as often on the basis of who's not busy as on who is perfectly qualified. This is both good and bad. A risk taker will have a field day trying different kinds of projects. A non-risk-taker will sweat and pine for a *Fortune* "500."

Small companies have as many disadvantages as advantages. However, what constitutes a disadvantage for one person may be an advantage for someone else, so you'll really have to make your own decision. These are the disadvantages cited by most of the people we interviewed.

1. *Paternalism cuts both ways.* While a paternalistic owner/manager may be more generous with cash, there is more truth than imagination in the stories you've heard about the ugly side of paternalism. Owners may demand and reward blind loyalty above competence. This happens in large corporations as well, but if you left a *Fortune* "500" to get away from a paternalistic manager that is small comfort.

A paternalistic manager may insist on managing not only the organization but your career, posing as an all-knowing guru. "I know what is best for you, trust me," is the stance. If you can't go along with this at least nominally, it will be a serious problem and may dictate a move out of the organization.

It's rarely easy to reason with someone who is convinced that he or she has your best interests at heart in the face of your spirited protests. Reasoning with someone who's listening to not only a different drummer, but one only he or she can hear, may put you into a career cul-de-sac. At the least you may break out in resentment and claustrophobia.

Family problems can drive you crazy, or at least out of the organization. All of the nepotism jokes television comedians tell are funny only when you don't have to live with them. No family is free of people who absolutely lack any business sense. Faced with a choice of welfare or employing them, many a paternalistic entrepreneur has "found a place" for the "special" one within an otherwise well-run company. It's more visible and aggravating in small companies than large ones only because there are fewer people and thus it's easier to spot the slugs.

2. *You often work harder and longer hours in a small company.* All of that camaraderie, not to mention team spirit and owner involvement, are achieved at a price. You will end up working harder and longer hours because there is usually more work to do. It's part of the mystic quality of the place. The nine-to-five set will sink here without a trace. They belong in maintenance organizations. This is to be expected and accounts largely for the owner's willingness to pay more money than could be expected in larger organizations. It's what bonuses are intended to insure. After all, he or she is getting more for the money. It's not a case of blind generosity.

3. *Office politics is frequently more deadly.* The grapevine in a small organization is instant and total. It's much like life in a small town that so many people leave to get away from. Fewer people in a smaller space concentrating on knowing almost everything about each other. There is no hiding place. The accompaniment to this is that the social togetherness of the employees after work is often daunting. If you long to turn your worn-out body into the local "Y" for rehabilitation after work every night, you'll find the hours spent drinking with boss and coworkers in a misguided (your opinion) attempt at comradeship very trying indeed. Small businesses demand better political and social skills.

Our experience indicates more people have abandoned an otherwise unblemished opportunity because of the physical and emotional togetherness and the probable consequences of nonparticipation than any other reason. Many people who've spent three to five years in a corporation in which attitude was not as important as performance find the adjustment impossible. If you decide to pursue the idea of working in a smaller company, this has got to be at the top of your checklist. Otherwise you'll end up unhappily trying to adjust to a style you can't hope to find tolerable, much less congenial.

The bottom line for success in a small business is that you must genuinely like the people you work with and for. Tolerance will not be enough because of the forced closeness. Even if you genuinely like all that you've met before you decide to take the job, ask yourself if you have enough flexibility to deal with enforced closeness. Not everybody does.

Roger, in a misguided belief that he could "get along with anybody" went to work for a small word processing equipment supplier. The owner was loud, jocular, and often offensive, in Roger's opinion. Despite the fact that Roger was earning about a third more than he had been making with the industry leader, he was job hunting in six months. He finally left before he had found another position. "I was with the guy ten hours a day, five days a week, and in two weeks I knew I hated him. It didn't take him more than a month to figure out that we didn't get along. The worst part was that he spent so much time wooing me. I had no specific complaints. I just disliked his style. In a small company the enforced closeness makes any incompatibility intolerable," Roger concluded.

4. *The instability may be real.* If the owner is an accomplished Johnny One-Note, the instabilty which many people imagine in small businesses may be very real. An owner/founder who is dedicated to producing one product or service superbly may not be able or willing to adapt his or her style or output enough to change with changing market conditions. In an unstable economy many one-idea people are likely to find themselves in trouble during market shifts. For an employee it may be like sitting on a time bomb. Unless you keep other options open, you may be surprised when the business begins to lose ground and management refuses to face the problem.

A second source of instability may be an owner's ego. If the owner decides that he or she isn't going to take advice because he or she has no need for it, this can be fatal to the business. An owner may also surround him- or herself only with clones, another source of fatality to the business. These conditions are especially likely to occur when the small company isn't publicly held. Then there may be no directors to force a note of reality into the owner's dream. Not only does this tend to unsettle other managers in the business, but it can cause nervous subordinates to flee literally without giving notice.

Elizabeth was won permanently back to the ranks of the *Fortune* "500" after two agonizing years watching the owner of a small flourishing advertising agency run her business into the ground. She had to stand by as the woman alientated every client, made the worst possible decisions, and drank enough to create a new Alcoholics Anonymous record. "I can't imagine going through that again," Elizabeth said. "It was like dying a slow death myself, watching the business fail. The worst part is that my former boss absolutely refused to get any kind of help, listen to any advice, to do anything but destroy the agency."

A third source may be the manager's lack of management skills. The more imaginative or technically talented, the less the owner may know or care about management skills. Many reports on small business failures identify a lack of managerial experience and talent as the primary cause, more important than the product or service or the financing. The more individualistic the owner the more likely he or she is to disregard the advice of people whose strengths are managerial rather than entrepreneurial. Beware the manager who refers to trained managers as "bureaucratic." Every business must have a few of those to keep the entrepreneurs from the business version of infanticide.

Lack of decent management may not kill the small business if the idea on which the business is based is sufficiently outstanding. It's always amazing how much mismanagement and even criminal neglect a business can withstand. Some seem to make money against all reason. The problem is not survival but your ability to cope with a situation that seems dangerous as a permanent condition. If you have a high tolerance for instability you can do very well in this environment. Think about it as a short-run learning experience; a way to boost your salary

quickly; and a way to start an IRA without necessarily planning to put in forty years at the company.

5. *You're expected to come equipped with the necessary skills
or train yourself.* For people who have worked for companies
that were scrupulous about training, the move to a small company can be like a swim in Lake Michigan in January. The
shock to the system is total, and it may even be fatal. It's not
just that smaller organizations don't believe in training except
for production line people. Frequently even that training is
haphazard. The problem may be that no one is even in charge
of explaining jobs well enough for you to understand what you
need training to do. The attitude is that versatility and willingness will make up for skill. Sometimes this is true. The problem
may be that combined with the organization's desire to get the
most out of its people there is also a philosophy of benign neglect.

You've heard the theory that the large organizations tend to
feed off the smaller ones. Some people call this "paying your
dues." The idea is supposed to be that a *Fortune* "500" would
be likely to hire someone who'd worked for a similar but much
smaller company in the same industry. It happens frequently
in the communications industry. You work for the university
publishing house or the small regional operation and eventually you've learned enough to assault one of the New York
giants. If you're interested in television presumably you begin
your career sweeping floors in Fargo and work your way back
to CBS in Chicago or New York.

What you hear less frequently, but it's equally as true, is that
small companies eagerly seek people who've been trained by
the *Fortune* "500." They don't always get them, and they rarely
want to pay them but they do seek them. From the small company's point of view, state of the art resides in the largest prac-
titioners in an industry.

Small companies see thesse employees as having been
trained at some other company's expense, always a plus. They
may figure the salary is a bargain because this is the case. If

you move from one small company to another you may find yourself less desirable. You may also find that all that you know you've taught yourself.

Even worse than training yourself is working for the organization that blindly enrolls its people in training courses of dubious quality run by national training outfits whose real strength is slick brochures, not skills development. It's usually a sign that no one has thought out what training can do or what this particular organization wants it to do. If you've ever been the victim of a three-day seminar that appears to be led by the one person who attended the previous edition of that seminar who seemed able to absorb 50 percent of the material and will work for the honor, you can appreciate how worthless many of these experiences are.

If you need training, you will need to choose a small company very carefully. Training need not be classroom-based; some of the best isn't. A good manager who can explain clearly, provide controlled experiences, and then give feedback, that is, a coach, can be quicker, and much better for you than the most carefully thought out three-month course. Don't expect to find a correlation between success as a manager and coaching skills. There may be, but if you need training, it's important to inquire about this up front. You may, if you are beginning your career now, want to spend a couple of years in a very large organization learning as much as you can at that organization's expense.

As a new employee with a tiny printing firm, Dan had problems finding out what he was supposed to do, much less how to do it. He did not even know enough about the business to ask the right questions. As the company grew, it became obvious that Dan's knowledge about the industry was superficial at best. He finally left for a much larger company where training might help him recoup. "I couldn't have moved up even in a booming business because there were so many gaps in my knowledge," Dan said. "When I left the owner had tears in his eyes because he liked me personally. Unfortunately I couldn't take the chance that he'd always be there to cover for me. I had to make sure that I learned enough about the industry to make it on my own."

Since training is critically important to how you do the job, especially when no formal system exists, it's up to you to ask the right questions about what the company can and can not provide.

What do they expect employees to know? A new college graduate may know a lot *about* a subject, marketing, for instance, but have no practical experience. Ask how much hands on experience the people who have done your job in the past have had.

Have any people failed in your job in the recent past? How did that happen? Beware the company that can cite several people who did what they propose to hire you to do and failed because they couldn't "cut" it. Usually that indicates one of two things. Either the company supplied inadequate information and training for the job up front or they consistently tried to pick people who did not need training. Either way you are putting yourself under a tremendous strain in thinking that you can figure out what needs to be done without some specific training from the organization. The difference between telling you what is to be done and training is that training covers not only what but how. The how part of the equation is the part most likely to cause you trouble.

Who will be responsible for training you? If this hasn't even occurred to the manager or owner, don't take the job. Osmosis may work in some situations but not this one. You can't hope to do the job unless you are getting specific, regular instruction. If you discover a vagueness here, probe further. If you meet a stone wall, you are putting yourself in a no win situation if you take the job.

Is there any kind of plan for training or even orienting new employees? One of the things personnel departments usually manage to sell management is the need for a systematic method for training people and even for bringing them on board initially. No small company will have a policy manual as elaborate as you'd expect to find at General Electric, but it should have some procedure, however informal, that resembles a plan for moving people from day one to full productivity.

These may seem very specific questions to ask, but your job success depends on them. It's one thing to assume a risk that the company will fail, but it's quite another to set yourself up by not minimizing all the risks you can. The problem of inadequate training is one you must deal with before you take the job.

6. *The company may be or may become vulnerable to take-over.* A company that happily went public five years ago may find that it is now every vulture's favorite target. If the prospect of management change unsettles you, you'll want to confine your examination of small companies to those that are not publicly held. This may have dangers as well if family members own the majority interest and they seem inclined to feuds.

7. *Just as you settle in, the company may grow so quickly it outgrows its owner or management.* Prosperity often seems to create as many problems for companies as poverty. A company that is charging along may outgrow both the conceptual and manageral skills of its owner. It's not news that the skills of entrepreneurs are very different from those of professional large-scale managers. A company stuck with one set when it needs another, has a serious time bomb ticking in its bowels. This is especially true when the owner can't face the problem. Growth may be unchanneled as everyone fights to put the company on an even keel. It may not be possible.

8. *There is little prestige outside the company's circle of admirers.* Prestige freaks wither in small companies. When you announce at a cocktail party who you work for and the response is, "Who?" it's not particularly an ego builder. If this could be or is a problem for you, you will not change your

mind in a small company no matter how much money you might earn. Do not kid yourself. If the need for a glamorous name, luxurious offices, a corporate art collection, and lots of *Wall Street Journal* coverage is important to you, stay away from small businesses. They are more likely to be long on dirt under the fingernails, old factory buildings, used furniture, and high profits. They'll sense how you feel anyway and that will be even worse for your career. Don't get into that sort of situation. You can't win.

You could change your mind if you had a very bad experience in a glamour company. Most people, our experience suggests, need several bad experiences before any other option seems attractive. Glamour is powerfully seductive. Even several bad experiences may not cure the truly prestige oriented.

9. *Benefits may be thin even as cash is more abundant.* Some of that extra cash you are getting may have to be diverted to providing a better quality health insurance coverage than the company provides. The company may even give no health or life insurance. Pension plans may be skimpy or nonexistent. This may epitomize insecurity for you. Keep in mind that most new companies don't put in pension plans, regardless of the tax advantages, until the owner/founder or the top management team begin to think about this issue in personal terms. If they all plan to die with their boots on, this might be quite a long time.

10. *Irrational quirks may be a hallmark of the organization.* These may vary from the merely irritating and mildly amusing to the arcane. Owner/founders find that half the fun of being owner/founders is the fun of doing what they please. Expect to see some fairly bizarre ideas enshrined as holy writ. For instance, one man with an extremely prosperous company wanted all of his employees, regardless of rank or function, sitting around him in a square so that they could pass papers back and forth. When he had three employees, it was no prob-

lem. When the company grew to ten, the passing process became a problem. He retained it as a memorial to less prosperous times even though productivity and morale suffered.

One retailer enjoyed counting the cash each night after his store had closed. When he had one small dress shop, this was no problem. When he had three in three suburban shopping centers, it was a burden. When he expanded to ten stores, it was impossible. He kept everyone in the company in suspense for six months while he decided if he could continue to expand if it meant that he couldn't count the cash each night. His reluctance to delegate this task didn't carry over to any other business function. It was a single quirk.

All of the desirable action is not in the small or the very large organization. There are certainly medium-sized ones as well. The trouble is that most frequently the medium-sized firms have the worst problems of both the very small and very large. There may be a slowing of growth as the organization comes to grips with its own past rapid growth. It may become increasingly vulnerable to merger or takeover. It may have the rigidity of a large organization without the large organization's top talent or financial resources. Like an adolescent, any industry's middle group of companies tend to mirror the problems that beset those on either side, often to greater intensity. The bottom line in most of these companies is that they'll have policies and a personnel department that aren't state of the art. Those are above all the enemies of salary maximization.

Finding the prosperous small business often resembles finding a needle in a haystack. The owner doesn't court publicity and may not particularly care to be known. He or she may put total energy into running the business with no thought of recruiting employees. It's unlikely the company will hire a recruiter and make the college circuit. Many of these companies rely on referrals and walk-ins for talent. They are usually very open and it's not hard to get to the right person once you have the name of the organization and know something about it.

Some things you could do to find these companies are as follows:

1. *Read the trade press in whatever industry you're interested.* The trade press is the one place the shy, small, wealthy company may turn up. (We've been told that the IRS reads the trade press religiously to see who's saying what to whom.) Owner/founders prefer recognition from people they know, that is, their peers to that from the public in general. They're more likely to share information or give interviews and releases to the trade press. Second, trade press people must have a genius for smelling out the comers in the industry. How else will they fill the pages of their magazines and newsletters every month? We've said it before but it's worth repeating. The trade press is the primary route to both career change and landing in a small prosperous company.

2. *Cultivate bankers and owners of small CPA firms.* A medium-size bank will know more about small businesses than a money center bank simply because that's the business of the smaller bank. It wants those companies as customers. The same is true of the small CPA firm. The owner is far more interested in picking up the audits on a couple of the businesses you're also interested in than trying to compete with the Big Eight for General Motors' business. You'll have to talk to quite a few bankers and CPA's before you turn up any company that seems to meet your needs. Printers and union business agents are also important sources of information depending on the industry.

3. *Talk to the Chamber of Commerce in the fastest growing community you know.* The small business owner is usually not simply a dues paying member in the local Chamber but attends a fair number of meetings. This is especially true if there are issues he or she is concerned about. The owner may be active as an officer. At the least he or she knows and is known by others in the organization. Talk with the Chamber's president about who he or she sees as the real movers in the size range and kind of business you are considering.

4. *Canvass your personal and professional contacts for people who work for small businesses.* Let everybody into the act from Great Aunt Bertha to the little girl who sells you Girl Scout cookies once a year. You'll be surprised as you thumb through your alumni directory and the directories of your professional and trade associations to see how many people you know or know of who work for companies you've never heard of. These are likely to be small businesses. Just as the people who work for Chrysler can name Chrysler's competitors, the people who work for Small Time Nut and Bolt know who their competitors are. These people are a primary resource in securing access to this hidden market.

5. *Let everybody know—if it's politically prudent—what you are looking for.* Sell them with your enthusiasm. Don't worry about those who try to discourage you or sell you their own experiences with small companies. One of the things that makes job hunters so tedious and inaccurate is that they always generalize from their own experiences. If you had a bad experience in a company headed by a certifiably insane owner/founder you tend to see all owner/founders as suspect. Keep your perspective and avoid those companies about which everyone's impressions is negative or even tentative.

6. *Expect this process to take a minimum of six months.* It may take as long as one year or more. Remember that these companies do little to make themselves visible to job hunters, or to anybody else. Even when you find a company that seems to fit your needs, you may not find the very opening you seek that minute. Keep after the company. Develop greater contact with the owner and some of the managers. Remember that more than in a big business personality can make or break you in the small company. Keep selling yourself. However, if you are not genuinely enthused about the people as well as the product and the environment don't take the job. If you keep selling and it's a good fit, a place can be found for you. This is especially true if you make it clear that that is what you want.

7. *Even if you find and go to work for a small business you love, retain your flexibility.* Set up an IRA and put in the maximum amount you can the first year. Remember that you may be here for some time and you don't need, nor should you consider, waiting to see how the job will work out. If there is no pension plan, start an IRA immediately. Expect to invest any bonus money that comes to you. You are in the business of providing your own financial security unless you think that you don't require any.

No Free Lunch

No company is truly ideal. The small business definitely doesn't fulfill the needs of many people who want an entirely different experience. For you it may be worth a try. After all, it is unlikely that the owner will try to tie you to the company with an iron-clad contract the first week on the job. Try it if it seems to meet your needs. There are always other options.

One of these may be learning all that you can about *small* business management and starting your own. You'll learn more about running a small business working in one than you will working for Exxon. Exxon operates on a lavish scale that no small business needs or could afford. If this has been in the back of your mind, the small business may provide an opportunity.

Our research indicates that more than 50 percent of the small businesses that have a good growth record are reasonably good places to work. If we seem to have put excessive emphasis on growth, it's because profitable growth provides a cushion, really a security blanket, for the small business, or the large one for that matter. Without that cushion, new managements often make the fatal mistake without realizing it.

Since small businesses are scattered all over the country, wherever an owner/founder happened to be, it's not nearly as difficult to work from where you are. If the burden of physically moving as well as changing jobs would be too unsettling, this is something to keep in mind.

12

Finding
the Large Organization
That's Keeping Pace

When Mary Ann considered her career on her thirtieth birthday, the first real period of taking stock for many people, she
saw several problems quite clearly. She had received a B.A. in
social studies eight years before and begun her career as a secretary. Now, although she was the highest paid secretary she
knew at $23,000 plus a $3,500 bonus, she could not help seeing
this job as a dead end. The only option she really saw was to go
back to school at night for an MBA. Fortunately for her, before she enrolled in a program at the local university, she decided to explore whether there might be any other way to move
into a management job.

To MBA or Not?

It wasn't just the prospect of two or three years of night
school that bothered her. She was more concerned about the
stories she'd heard and read that indicated that unless she attended a MBA program in the top ten, which was not available
where she lived, there was no guarantee she'd be able to turn

the degree into dollars. Smart woman. She had discovered a hidden truth that the admissions officers of most business schools, especially those started in the past ten years to meet the "demand," don't like to talk about. An MBA from a less than stellar institution can depress, rather than increase, your earning power, particularly when you are over 30. (You have to feed an aggressive admissions counselor from a second-rate school several martinis to get him or her to tell the truth.)

She put the MBA idea on the back burner and began to examine other ways of moving up. She knew that her boss, desperate as he was to keep her, had gotten her the highest salary increase possible out of his boss. There was no way to justify paying one secretary almost $7,000 more than any other in the company, even to keep the vice president of sales happy. She was bumping her head against a ceiling that only inflation could move up.

Mary Ann's boss was determined to keep her as his secretary. That's why he'd fought so hard for her salary increases. She could expect no help from him in moving internally. Since the company was small and highly technical, she would need an engineering degree to move into management anyway. She began to think of a move outside the company, possibly to a much larger company, where there would be more room to move. While she lived in a large city she had little knowledge of any of the large firms headquartered there. How to pick likely candidates seemed the problem.

Mary Ann's reason to consider a larger organization is not the only one. There are a number of valid reasons to make a move to a company with thousands of employees and a policy manual the size of the Manhattan white pages.

The Good News

Your problem is to be sure you understand the potential advantages and disadvantages before you job hunt. This is not something you can afford to learn from experience. For our purposes a large company is one of the *Fortune* "500" or one of the largest in its industry.

1. *You need state-of-the-art training.* The larger the organization the more likely it is to have a training department worthy of the name. Instead of a manager providing a cursory overview of the subject, the company has structured programs, which include both classroom and field experience. Some of these companies may include the assignment of a mentor as part of the training process or send you for industry-sponsored training periodically.

WARNING: In bad times, the training budget for everyone but production line workers and salesmen is likely to be raided. Only the most prosperous companies will continue broad-based training in a recession. Training can be a political football. The training department may be funded according to how valuable management believes the function to be. If management thinks people should learn on the job the training department may not do skills training. It will then be confined to human relations programming. If management thinks that all human relations programming is "touchy-feely," it will do skills training. Changes in top management will be reflected in the training area as in every area of personnel.

The best training operation is one in which managers not only send people to programs but in which everyone in the organization is expected to participate in some kind of regular updating. For instance, the managers of all data processing and word processing areas are expected to attend regular meetings on new technology. All managers are expected to attend not only their trade/association meeting annually but regular association-sponsored updating on management techniques. In other words, the company is committed to fighting voluntary obsolescence among its employees. Usually the more technology is vital to the company, the more they train.

A well-run training operation will also provide training and orientation for those people promoted from within, not just those recruited from outside. The people doing the training are a mixture of line managers rotated for six months to a year to work in training and professionals whose careers are as trainers. Despite the bad mouthing you often hear about former school teachers in training departments, that's a plus. The one thing a teacher can be expected to know is how to organize and cut up information into digestible chunks. Training is teaching in a different environment.

If the training is confined to just a few people at the top of each internal pyramid, someone like Mary Ann would be left out. If you need training, you'll have to look carefully and talk to a great many people before you discover what the training practice—as opposed to philosophy—really is.

2. *You don't really have a concrete long-term goal.* Let's face it. Every time a friend describes his or her job you can imagine yourself doing it especially if it's hinted that it pays more or has the potential to pay more. You don't know what you want potential for, you're just sold on the idea. You are available to the highest bidder. Somehow you escaped the parental programming which got many people at age five to say, "I want to be a ... when I grow up." The largest organization you can find in an industry that interests you somewhat can provide a bird's eye view of many possibilities. This move may be necessary before you can make a commitment.

There is no substitute when trying to make a career decision for working at a variety of jobs in a somewhat organized structure. That is, you need to be able to test your skills in a controlled situation rather than in the small business with its more haphazard assignment system. Especially if you tend to shun the risks involved in throwing yourself into a new job with a hope and a prayer, the largest company can provide both plan and opportunity for moving around.

In the 1980s you'll see many more companies engaged in cross-functional job rotation. Translated from the native jargon this means that you will come into an organization with a particular set of skills and you will work with those skills for an initial period: usually one to three years. At that point you may begin to move through a series of jobs that provide related experience and are shorter term assignments. The company's idea is that if you learn a variety of jobs you'll be less bored and therefore less likely to leave. They'll have a more flexible work force. This can only happen in organizations that have a great many jobs related by a common core of skills, that is, very large companies.

There can be salary opportunities here as you move around provided you move up at the same time. If all of your moves are in the same salary range, you are getting training and an overview but you're falling behind financially. If may not be possible to turn what you've learned into dollars in that organization. You may need to relocate to a competitor's shop.

3. *The company offers a particular benefit you need which is worth a great many untaxed dollars.* You need $7,000 worth of caps on your rapidly deteriorating teeth. The largest companies in your town have a very comprehensive dental insurance. You want to finish your degree in night school or start a masters program, and the largest company provides the most generous tuition remission. Or you have a child in need of delicate, elective surgery, which your present employer's health policy doesn't begin to cover; or you personally need some kind of expensive medical treatment. Unless you make a tremendous salary having your employer pay for medical bills is always better than paying yourself and taking the tax deduction. The more you make the higher your bracket and the more valuable the nontaxed benefits your employer provides can be. This can be as good as or better than a substantial raise the first year, but only that one year.

4. *You need the security or the feeling of security the large company provides.* You have looked around and you perform best when working for a company with maximum stability. You can't see yourself in an environment which seems "will-o-the-wisp" as long as you are solely responsible for you. This may stem from unhappy job experiences in the past. It may be that you need some place to park at least temporarily. A large

company can fill this need nicely. Even if the security is more imagined than real, you may do fine if it helps you perform better.

5. *You want the glimmers of prestige that fall on you from your association with the big company.* The small advertising firm might pay more, but who has ever heard of it outside of the advertising community? You think you might be able to turn the association with the prestigious company into dollars down the road and in the meantime you do enjoy the reflected glory. You're willing to trade dollars for glory.

6. *The company indexes all salaries to the CPI (Consumer Price Index).* The CPI is actually a little ahead of inflation. This, you will remember from Chapter 2, is what Social Security and a number of government pensions are indexed to. CPI indexing means that you automatically get periodic raises as the CPI goes up. This is generally a big-company phenomena and only in a union shop. Usually the nonunion people get these cost of living increases because the union won it for its members. Management makes this concession to the nonunion help because otherwise there will be no gap between union and nonunion salaries.

The number of companies that have CPI indexing is not large. You may find one in your community by simply asking people you know. If you do there is likely to be either a waiting list of people wanting to work there or some talk at the company of dropping the CPI provision. If it's a strongly union shop, the union will fight this move. If, however, the system must be retained for the union, it doesn't necessarily have to be for the nonunion people. The company may review its compensation for nonunion people and go entirely to a merit system.

Indexing can be an asset to you if you come in at a market-level salary. If you accept a job for below market, indexing will move you up more quickly but usually not bring you up to market immediately. If you stay there long enough, you'll actually surpass market. If you are in need of cash quickly, this can be an asset to you for a few years. In fact, it may be your best strategy.

7. *The company is organized in discreet divisions but with some interaction between them.* If the right hand doesn't know or care what the left is doing it defeats the purpose (for you) of being in a very large organization. You want to be able to move around with some ease, not as if you were moving from company to company.

One of the principal assets of the large company is that it will almost certainly post job openings. If the openings are real and not just posted by managers after they've been filled from the department to comply with company policy, this can be helpful to you in moving from area to area. It will depend on how much power any individual manager has to thwart the process. If the boss can delay a transfer for six months to a year because it would be inconvenient for him or her, the transfer system will move like molasses. This is not particularly helpful to you. If, on the other hand, there is lots of internal movement, each move provides an opportunity to get more money.

8. *A well-run personnel department could be an asset.* Personnel could actually provide some mediation and counseling services for employees. They may be mandated to publish salary ranges and make other kinds of very important information available. They may be able to represent you within the organization and actually help you locate some openings you would not ordinarily hear about before they are posted. At the least, they might intercede on your behalf. It's highly unlikely that such a department exists in very many large organizations. If you think you might need any of these services, you'll want to talk with other employees about the quality of personnel services before you need them.

9. *The company is growing so quickly some of the usual rigidity has been eliminated.* In the scramble to control and manage growth, the need for, and even the possibility of, using all established procedures has been eliminated. Managers in their scramble to fill openings and keep jobs covered are more will-

ing than usual to negotiate and to bend the scales and make exceptions. This may be a temporary phenomenon, and you'll have to be prepared to jump when you see things heating up. Rapid growth in the largest companies may be seasonal. It may be released on a new product just coming on the market. It may be the result of acquisition. How the growth came about is more important in terms of opportunity for rapid advancement than the mere fact of growth.

If you want to look at the growth of a particular company or all of those in a particular industry go to the library and get the *Fortune* "500" list (or *Fortune* "200" or "100") depending on industry. You need the lists for the past five years. Compare gross sales or income over that period and figure the percentage increase or decrease. You might also want to chart ratio of employees to gross income. If the organization generates more dollars per employee, this is good management but not necessarily fertile ground for job hunting.

10. *The company has an outstanding pension plan.* You want to retire at 55 rather than 65 so that you can begin your second career. A very large company is more likely to have provisions for this than a small one simply because its pension plan is long established, amply funded, and reasonably well managed. In an owner/founder business, the pension plan may still be under discussion when you're ready to retire because the owner doesn't want to retire and therefore sees no need to encourage anyone else to either.

The pension plan may be set up for earlier than ten-year vesting. The closer to retirement age you are, the more dependent you would be on a pension, the more you'll need to investigate what the company's policies are. A company with a 30 years' service-and-out clause could be beneficial to you if you are very young (under 35). Otherwise, it can mean that you won't get the maximum benefit from that organization. Tread carefully here. Remember that pension plans can be changed infinitely up to the time you retire and are an active participant.

The Bad News

As with every other thing we've discussed there are as many, maybe more, potential drawbacks and hence reasons not to choose a large organization as reasons to do so.

1. *The sense of security you feel may be more illusory than real.* There have got to be many individual and collective moments of black dread in the automobile companies right now. There are, no doubt, people in the railroad industry who worry about the future. There is no absolute security, although this has not been so clear until some of the seemingly most stable companies in the country got into trouble.

While the savings and loan institutions may be insured vis-á-vis their depositors, their employees may not share the sense that they have nothing to lose. One hears that these people are putting money into money market funds. There have been some bailouts for large banks as well as other kinds of businesses. The fact that the building looks solid creates an illusion that may or may not have a basis in fact. You may get there only to find out that a major reorganization is about to begin. Size and stability are not necessarily soul brothers.

2. *The company may have hardening of the arteries.* The company may resist change in every form. It may be as bureaucratic as the federal government and even less likely to change, if that's possible. The management may be so comfortable that someone to the right of Howard Ruff would be considered radical. Size and flexibility are often at opposite ends of the spectrum. There is no necessary relationship. Management, wherever trained, may see individual security as the collective goal. If you look here for the fast track, you're not going to find it. The company values longevity above everything. Beware the organization that really does fill jobs exclusively from within. That much inbreeding is as likely to produce a mentally retarded management team as genius. This may be difficult to detect if the company runs regular employment ads. Who do

they hire? Are they using the ads as good faith search ads to show the government they are attempting to recruit minorities and women or do they actually hire people?

3. *The company may strictly enforce its salary schedules.* It may feel that across-the-board increases, regardless of merit, are much cheaper in the long run because they entirely eliminate the need to negotiate anything with anybody. In the end, this alone may put the big guy on the ropes, but that may be long after you've decided to look elsewhere.

The company may decide to pay its version of competitive salaries without anything approaching adequate research. Nor will it be amenable to your research results. It's very hard to sell salary research to some top managements because the results seem so intangible. As one president said, "Just look in the paper and see what our competitors are paying. That's how you set salaries."

4. *You may get lost in the masses.* Unless you have a sponsor or make visibility your most important goal, you may lose out to those who are easier to spot. It requires more planning and work and a greater facility with office politics to make sure that you are visible to the right people. It also takes quite sophisticated research to find out who the right people are! The need to keep the nonproductive and the people with titles on in jobs where they can't hurt themselves or anyone else, coupled with government regulations, may obscure who really can help you.

5. *It may be hard ball office politics.* Life among the politically upwardly mobile is often quite unpleasant unless you enjoy politics and have developed good skills. The politics may center on issues in which you can't compete. If every other person at your level has a Harvard MBA and you don't, it will be more noticeable. Conformity is a hallmark of the large organization. Some almost seem to signal that they'd clone if given the opportunity. If you are a doctrinaire nonconformist, you will be miserable in such an organization. Unlike the owner/manager who confronts you with your shortcomings,

you may simply be sidetracked because you don't fit in. If you are determined to live a particular lifestyle at odds with the lifestyle you see in the corporations you consider, you are asking for failure. There is a reason all of those people are dressed by Brooks Brothers. If you are allergic to the look, it will be an unhappy experience for you. You are not going to change the system until you have the power to do so. You won't get that power until you've learned to feel very comfortable in the corporate uniform.

Managers may feel strong needs to show instant results. Each person's career can rest on what happens today regardless of the long-range consequences. Don't underestimate the damage to your career of one small setback in such an environment.

If you are working for a workaholic you will have to show the same tendencies to survive. If you lack these and can't fake them, it's political suicide. Style is very important, and many departments have a distinct style which is almost mandatory for those who want to succeed there.

6. *The company is selling prestige.* Are you a potential buyer? No matter how long you worked there or how well you did it's unlikely you would make as much money as in a less well-known place. The company has never had a people shortage because the people dazzled by its reputation are standing in line. If you are one of them, keep in mind that they are compensating people with prestige as much as money. It's unlikely that a small company could get away with this.

Finding the Stars

Where can you find the exceptional large organization? Certainly they are more visible, more talked about than smaller organizations. Ever mindful of stockholder relations and public image, however, they are inclined to manage the information available through the media. No company can manage its financial information if publicly held, but it can obscure the facts about the quality of work life inside.

Trade and professional associations can supply former employees. There is nothing like someone who left one of these behemoths in the area that interests you to give you some inside dope on what went on. You want to find out two things. How was money distributed and how often? Who received the best increases? If you don't fit the profile of who's getting the best dollars, it may not be worthwhile to change. You might also want to ask if the former employee thinks there are any time bombs in the company which might shorten its life. Even secretaries and clerks can see some of the suicidal strategies management uses. It doesn't take a senior vice president.

Talk to some securities analysts. If they work in that industry, they may know more about the company's actual behavior even than a former employee.

Talk to search firm people. What has been their experience with the larger companies in town? How long have the people they placed there stayed? Let these people know that you might be a candidate but that you are looking for information at this point. Some will talk and some won't. If you're in an area to feed them candidate names, they may help. If not, you'll have to look for information elsewhere.

Do a 5- or 10-year literature search. See what has happened in the past. This can be done very quickly if you read only those articles that promise summaries of business activity. Has there been anything wholly unfavorable published in the past 5 years? Are there any dire predictions for the industry as a whole?

What are the possibilities of a merger, takeover, or reorganization? You've seen the literature but you need to know what knowledgeable people predict for the future. Big is not necessarily safe. It may be that the company is even vulnerable to being subdivided. How would a divestiture affect your career? There is no such thing as a corporate secret. If the idea of a major change in the company's structure has crossed the mind of anyone higher in the organization than the mailroom manager (often an excellent source of information if properly cultivated) there is a trail to that story you can pick up.

Managing Constant Change

Remember that nothing is permanent. You are probably aware by now that you aren't going to find the happy hunting ground where you can settle in and relax. You'd be more comfortable if you concentrated on one- to three-year plans rather than trying to put yourself in a place to stay 30. That mind set, regardless of the size of the company, can reduce your buying power. All you need do is develop the mentality of someone determined to hang on, and everyone in your organization will see you as a patsy. Company loyalty is the enemy of salary maximization. Only if you perform better than average, have good political skills, and appear ready to move if dissatisfied, are you likely to command a market level salary. The meek may inherit the earth but not any part of it that could be said to be profitable.

13

Looking to the Future

It's been almost 10 years since you graduated from college or completed your education. You're progressing nicely in your career and you are being paid at, or close, to market for your efforts. At this particular moment you have no complaints, at least none worth acting to correct. What else do you need to do to keep current so that you can avoid some of the economic bumps in the road? Just because you and the company both seem in sync today does not have any predictive value for tomorrow.

All Work, No Play

On the other hand, it's rather a joyless process to spend most of your spare time on research and updating especially when you may not need the information for months or years. The temptation is to let this go for as long as there's no critical need. Hence here are some quick-and-dirty ways to maximize your information without spending your life assembling.

Train yourself to clip articles from magazines and newspapers. Teach yourself to read with scissors. You're looking for every fact, every prediction, every scrap of information which impacts on your career decisions. Dump these unread into a file folder and keep them handy for the time you'll need them. Anything three years old or older can probably be dispensed with. Scanning the *Wall Street Journal* does not take long when you are looking for very specific kinds of information. You will want to clip some or all of the following kinds of information.

1. Industry forcasts that cover the industry or specific kind of business you work for or wish to work for.

2. Any predictions, reports, or speculations about your own company or its largest competitors.

3. General economic information about your age group particularly if you are part of the baby boom crowd. How are your peers doing overall?

4. Starting salary information for jobs like the one you have. Be sure the article tells where and when the information was collected. Without these facts it's fairly worthless because the information may be too old.

5. Success stories about people in your line of work. How did they move up rapidly or move from one organization to another? Do they know any tricks you could use?

6. Stories that indicate that management values in your industry are changing. For instance, if you begin reading about quality of work life and management's interest in promoting worker satisfaction you can be sure that fairly soon your own organization will be talking about these issues. Would any of them help you or your career?

7. Stories that indicate shifts in consumer tastes. If you work for a package goods company, you've got to be interested in the weakening of consumer brand loyalty. What does the rising sales curve for supermarket generic products mean to your career? Is this likely to make it harder or easier for you to keep pace with inflation?

8. Stories on the rise and fall of the population group to which you belong—women, middle class men, minorities, people over 40, etc.

Write out your career goals for the next five years. Career goals should include three things.

1. How much longer will you stay at your present job? This may mean you'll look for an internal job rather than a move out of the organization. If you know that you are fighting boredom now, this will naturally color your decisions.

2. How often are you prepared to move? If it makes you very uncomfortable to contemplate life as a gypsy, this should be included in your career goals. One of your career goals may be to stay where you are for at least three years. Just be sure you're willing to pay financially for this decision.

3. Are you expecting any sudden expenses or personal crises? The birth of a child could fill both conditions. This should be incorporated into your plans. Men and women who want to give more time to a new family, or an old one, may contemplate staying longer in a less demanding job.

Review this once a year before you and your boss do a performance or salary review. If you do this each year and find that it's exactly the same when you review it twelve months later, you have a problem. You are stagnating. Movement is doubly important for those who want to maximize salary.

Solicit employer support not only for your national and local dues for your trade or professional association but for the monthly meetings as well. Systematically go through the group's local directory and make sure that you've met everyone who could be even remotely useful to you. Don't let more than two months go by without attending a meeting. You don't have to stay for the speaker if it's not interesting, but you should be there without fail during the cocktail hour.

Raise your visibility where you now work. You can't avoid office politics. Even if you are planning an immediate move, practice your skills. Political skills have as much to do with how much money you make as the skills you actually use to do the job. If you disdain politics, you're making a mistake. Nobody can swim against that tide unless he or she is the mad scientist type so critical to the company that any kind of behavior will be tolerated. There are very few of these.

Take a course in negotiation and practice, practice, practice. Do your shopping at garage sales and street fairs and bargain with everybody. Set up practice sessions before any critical negotiations. Don't ever go into any negotiating session cold and rely on your wits to carry you. If you know the theory and practice of first-rate negotiation the process will carry *you*. This is what you want and need. No one, under pressure, is able to shoot from the hip effectively. Preparation is critical, and it must be practiced and kept polished. There is no need to spend large amounts of time on record keeping and research if you drop the ball when you present the results.

Take a course in financial planning and use what you learn. You may find that investing money is almost more interesting than making it. You are totally responsible for your own financial future. How will you live at 80? That's the worst possible time to be poor. The statistics suggest you will live into your 70's even if you never exercise and smoke. Who will support you?

As you grow older, increase, don't decrease, the sheer number of your business contacts. Remember that job hunting is a numbers game. At 25 you need 200 contacts to generate 10 live job leads. At 35 you need 400 contacts to generate 10 live job leads. At 45 you need 600 contacts to get the same result. The tendency is for people to slack off in their forties rather than increase their network building. You can't afford to do this unless you have a very wealthy relative who's already died and left you his or her fortune for which you are marking time until you collect.

Keeping Files

There are certain essential records you need to keep. Filing and record keeping are probably not your favorite jobs but once you get your system to the maintenance stage you'll be very glad you got started. The maximum time you need to spend doing this per month is an hour. Between filing orgies simply put all of the things to be filed in a box or basket.

All financial records should be in the same file drawer. A two-drawer file cabinet will do it for most people. You need all of your federal and state income tax returns back to the beginning of your full-time work. This has nothing to do with a fear of the IRS. They don't go back that far unless something is radically wrong. You are going to use these to chart your income over time against taxes paid and inflation.

Keep all stock transactions and records. If you have money market funds, keep the monthly reports. Keep everything that has to do with cash and income and outgo. That's how you're going to chart your lifestyle; that is, if you remember Chapter 3, you're going to try to determine what percentage of your income you're really living on. Let's hope it's not something like 110 percent. It should be between 80 and 85 percent.

Keep all of your pension records together both from your own private pension investments such as IRA and Keogh and whatever a company fund provides. Most people toss out the company's annual pension report and that is a mistake. If any changes are made in that plan, you'll be the last to know if you're one of those people who shove company reports, unread, into a file, or, worse yet, throw them away.

Put all of your salary market research into the same file drawer. It should be with your general financial records. Your salary survey information is probably most critical to your ability to get more money out of present, past, and future employers. Therefore you'll need to update this once a year. Keep each year's finished report in a separate folder. Your salary research should include:

1. Names of all contacts including telephone numbers, from whom you secured reliable information.

2. Anything unusual you discovered. For instance, was one

or more of the companies surveyed very much under market or very much over market?

3. Any red flags you discovered or any issues that popped up which require further research. For instance, you found that market in your field is leveling off. This may indicate that there are surplus competent people or a decline in demand.

4. Any companies that particularly impressed you whom you'd want to investigate should you decide to move.

Be sure to put any clips from magazines and newspapers that bear on your research into this file. (Transfer them from your general clip file.) This will make it easier to go through for a quick search should that be necessary. Keep monthly CPI and other measures of the rate of inflation so that you can make sure your forecasts are accurate.

In the other drawer of your file cabinet you want to keep your career plans. It's not easy to become a planner when you've been used to shooting from the hip. In the 1980s it's necessary. One of the things you'll find most helpful is keeping a work journal. This is described in detail in the book, *Office Politics: Seizing Power/Wielding Clout* by this author, released in June 1981 by Warner Paperbacks. Chapter Two explains the process. The basic idea is that you will do your own performance appraisals regularly. Keep copies of all performance reviews regardless of the degree of truth from your point of view. Performance reviews are political not productivity records. You should be keeping your own productivity measures.

Coming Attractions

Productivity is going to be a major issue in the 1980s and it's not going to be confined to blue collar people who do measurable tasks. Everyone is going to be subject to measurement. It's important to find out what standards are, or are likely to be, used in your area to measure productivity. Are you doing more, with better results than you did last year? How would you rate your own performance? One of the infallible signs that your career is in trouble is the fact that you are slowing down and producing less. If the quality is also diminishing, you should be thinking about a different work theatre or even a different career.

What are the 1980s likely to be like for people who are not prepared as we've described?

There is already a psychology of fear among people when they talk about money and salary negotiation. At seminars, we hear people talking about being "grateful" for a raise because, "I could be replaced in a minute." What this indicates to us is either a lack of self-confidence or else a fairly skillful campaign on the part of management to convince people they are lucky to be employed. Given the generally declining level of productivity across the boards in this country if you are more productive than the average worker, you are not lucky to be employed. You are earning what you are paid, probably more.

More people seem less eager to negotiate for money and more likely to take whatever they are offered. This is a totally self-defeating strategy. People can afford to coast in good times, not bad.

Expect many companies to drop their cost of living indexing regardless of what index they use. The trend is to strictly merit increases with 75 percent of the raise pool reserved for those who perform in the top 20 percent, that leaves a mere 25 percent of the pool for 80 percent of the people. In fact, those who perform at a rate of average or below will not get anything.

Expect more companies to offer more benefits instead of more money. This may or may not help you. If the company offers tuition for the children of employees and you're childless this won't help; also if the company had dental insurance and you've never had a cavity. While a company may offer a wide range of benefits that it hopes hits most employees' needs, you should not be seduced by this unless your needs are being met. Life insurance policies are wonderful if you live dangerously and have beneficiaries. They are not a benefit if you don't. Remember that the kind of term insurance offered by most organizations has no cash value and certainly isn't portable.

What a company hopes to sell employees and what the employees can and will buy is always at odds. This is especially true in dual career marriages. If both you and your spouse have careers and carry family health insurance coverage you'll probably still only be able to benefit from one policy. The rest of the coverage you can't benefit from is wasted.

As more companies explore less universal benefits, paternity leave, day care services or allowances, and transportation allowances, there may be tax exempt benefits for you. Our only concern is that you not make a career decision on the basis of total benefits without separating out those which do not now and may never benefit you. The bottom line is spendable cash. Don't trade off cash for benefits you can't use.

Expect more, and more frequent, job description changes. If there's any way to get people to work harder for the same money, a great many companies are looking for it. Your job is to see that you are watching out for your own interests. Unless you can sell the idea that you and the company ought to split the savings, you may end up doing two jobs for the price of one.

Think of yourself as a perpetual job hunter. If you are not constantly on the lookout for opportunities, it takes longer to turn them up when you need to make a quick move. There's unlikely to be two years' notice given when a company starts sinking. You may need to move in a week, a month, or two months. This may require a major adjustment in your thinking if you have always secretly longed for a safe berth. Make the adjustment if you are interested in your career.

Expect some companies to talk about quality of work life at the expense of money. It's wonderful to have a fun job that you can't wait to go to every day. The bottom line is still the net on payday. If the company is truly in a bind and can't raise salaries it may resort to any number of substitutes. As long as inflation continues, only the nontaxed benefits come close to substitutes. It's not a plot. The issue of the quality of work life may have some validity for some people at some kinds of jobs. For people struggling to make ends meet it's a luxury.

Top management is as vulnerable as you are to change. Your boss and those above him or her in the hierarchy are as vulnerable to change as you. Expect that disquiet to be acted out in greater political activity. You may be surprised to see people spending more time on politics and less time on work. This will be a career problem for them so don't follow suit. In most organizations, the need to seem to be more than ordinarily productive may mute the effect of politics though it won't lessen the number of people who use politics instead of productivity.

Nonprofit organizations will be especially unstable. Inflation is harder on any organization that cannot pass its direct costs on to its clients or customers as quickly or almost as quickly as these rise. If those clients or customers are used to a particular size increase, they may resist very strongly. Since nonprofits, like other service operations, are people intensive, the tendency is to cut people. After all, there is a bottom line on how many paper clips and pens can be cut. If you are truly dedicated to the nonprofit sector, you will need to take to heart most of the advice in this chapter, especially that about seeing yourself as a permanent job hunter.

Most organizations will be on a fat-reducing diet. If you've always longed for an era in which only the productive who can prove it will survive this may be your best period. Most companies are, or will soon, develop an obsession with cost and people cutting. They are bound to whack out some of the productive as well as the less productive, but they are at least gunning for the less productive. Cost-cutting ideas will have an attentive audience. It may be worth promotions to think efficiency.

Our purpose isn't doom and gloom. Life in a monastery, while presumably secure, does not hold out a lot of excitement. Ditto the Motherhouse of a cloistered order of nuns. You can do well in the 1980s provided you understand what the economic variables are, and not just now but at the time you need to negotiate.

Finally, don't buy any promises that there is or can be one hot/hot career or one hot strategy for the 1980s. The key is flexibility in your planning and your thinking. That's what will help you beat inflation and still enjoy what you do for a living.

INDEX

650.1 Kennedy, Marilyn
KEN   Moats

Salary strategies

DATE			